Rosemary Penfold lives with her husband of thirty-five years not far from where she grew up, in the heart of Somerset. She has four children, eleven grandchildren and two great-grandchildren. She is still close to her extended Romany family who meet regularly for family gatherings. Although 'settled', her Romany roots mean she is still a Gypsy at heart.

Rosemary was a finalist for the People's Author competition on *The Alan Titchmarsh Show*, and her first book, *A Field Full of Butterflies*, went on to become a *Sunday Times* bestseller.

A Posy
of
Wild Flowers

ROSEMARY PENFOLD

1 3 5 7 9 10 8 6 4 2

Copyright © Rosemary Penfold 2012

A CIP catalogue record for this book
is available from the British Library.

ISBN: 9781409138372

Typeset by Input Data Services Ltd,
Bridgwater, Somerset

Printed in Great Britain by
Clays Ltd, St Ives plc

The Orion Publishing Group's policy is to use papers that
are natural, renewable and recyclable and made
from wood grown in sustainable forests. The logging and
manufacturing processes are expected to conform to the
environmental regulations of the country of origin.

This is a work of non-fiction, and the events it recounts are true.
However, the names and certain identifying characteristics of
some of the people who appear in its pages have been changed.
The views expressed in this book are the author's own.

www.orionbooks.co.uk

I watched a bumble bee today
I saw its coat, soft, black and gold,
I felt the tears start in my eyes
I remembered you just three years old.
You stood and watched the bumble bee
How beautiful you thought he was
You bent to stroke his furry back
Then he stung your hand without a cause.
You found too late that beauty is not always as it seems
And sometimes hides a cruelty that cannot be believed.

Thanks

Grateful thanks to all at Orion Books; you have made a dream come true. Huge thanks especially to Luigi, Amanda, Celia, Nicki, Juliet and Sophie Mitchell for helping me to have the confidence to have another go when I was so doubtful that I could do it again! Thank you so much to my daughter Sarah for all the time she has spent in helping me and without whom I could not have written this book. Thank you to all who wrote to tell me how much they enjoyed *A Field Full of Butterflies* and sent cards and flowers. Some even stopped me in the street to ask if I was 'the lady who wrote *that* book!' What a joy it has all been at a time in my life when I expected to be taking it easy.

I would especially like to mention Ivy Willets-Brunt who sent me a truly beautiful poem that she had written entitled 'The Gypsy'. The final sentence, 'What a loss not to see him again,' brought tears to my eyes. It was so much like my father and Granfer. My parents, Edwin and Mary, are no longer with us, neither are my grandparents, Edwin and Mary Ann. They would have been so proud of my achievement, as would my late brother, Nelson, and as Teddy and Chris are. Granny in Town would have been full of pride. She was always so kind to us, sending all sorts of delicious treats, which we all appreciated. What a lovely lady she was – and what a cook! The day she gave a small girl the gift of a box of 'jewels' has always been a wonderful memory. Thank you all once more.

Rosemary

Granfer's Advice

They pulled my hair and called me names, they gals I didn't
    know,
The tears they comes into my eyes, but I never lets 'em flow,
At night I layed awake in fear and I'd shake from 'ead to toe
    – Granfer said,
'Don't bother with they gadje gals, don't pay they no mind,
Praps you'm different but why care? Just leave they tears
    be'ind,
You be you, my little flower, wild flowers smell as sweet
As they be'ind the garden gate, tho' they be bright an' neat,
Praps one day will come a time when they gadje gals will
    say,
"We knowed 'er once, when we was young,
How I wish we'd let 'er play".'

1

Traveller's Joy

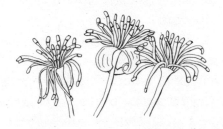

The day was very hot and the bus was crowded. Every window was closed. I sat down thankfully in one of the last vacant seats and a young woman who I knew by sight sat next to me.

'Phew! What a squash!' she sighed.

I nodded but said nothing. I was hot and tired and not in the mood for small talk. As we neared home the bus was just crawling along. Passengers started craning their necks to see why. Some passengers voiced their annoyance aloud.

'What's the hold up?' someone asked.

'It's the Gyppos!' someone replied nastily.

As the bus slowly edged forward, I could see five or six very expensive-looking trailers (caravans) that were trying to pull onto a large empty lot at the side of the road. Suddenly there was an explosion of rage.

'Dirty Gyppos!'

It was the woman sitting next to me who hissed this

venomous outburst. Her eyes full of hate and rage, she added to it.

'They think they own the land!'

'Yes!' Another agreed, sneering.

'Thieves and robbers, leaving their rubbish for others to clear up. Dirty lot.'

Righteous indignation welled up in me and I could not stop myself.

'Well,' I ventured, quietly, 'they don't look dirty to me. In fact, they look as spotless as their trailers. They must have cost a great deal.'

'Yeah,' someone yelled from the back, 'stolen, I expect!'

I turned to the woman sitting beside me. I recognised her only slightly as I had exchanged a 'hi' or a smile if I saw her in the local shops. She had always seemed very pleasant.

'How can you make comments about people you don't even know? In fact, I don't think you would recognise a Gypsy if one sat next to you, would you?'

'I would,' she replied. 'In fact I would rather stand than sit next to a dirty Gypsy!'

'Why didn't you then?' I continued.

'What?' She looked bemused.

'I am one of those "Gyppos" and you have been sitting next to me for the last half hour, but I won't mind if you never do so again.'

Her face was a picture and she hurriedly made her way to the front of the bus to alight. All went very quiet until a young woman a few seats away leaned towards me.

'I am so sorry,' she said, 'I wanted to speak up. I lived near a Gypsy camp when I was a child and I played every day with the children until they moved away. It broke my heart when they did. I learned to share from them as they always shared what little they had with me. I still miss them now.'

Reflecting on that horrible scenario later that evening, I realised how little most people know about Romany people. I also realised how much things had changed for them since my childhood. The people I had seen that afternoon, with their expensive trailers, bore little resemblance to the people I had grown up with, or the life we had lived back then. Although gypsies in those days were hard-working, they had little in the way of this world's goods. They rejoiced with each other if fortune smiled on any of them and mourned alongside those who suffered tragedy. They were always ready to lend a helping hand.

I remembered how our *vardoes* (wagons) were so simply built, but strong and warm. Each was brightly painted, with the little window to one side, and was a triumph of organisation. They had to be or we would have lived in chaos. We learned from an early age to put what few possessions we had tidily away so that we had plenty of room to move around.

The woman on the bus had said she would have recognised a Gypsy anywhere, but obviously she hadn't. Her preconceived ideas had misled her and probably many others. Times had certainly changed since I was a young girl, living with my extended family in the Gypsy encampment on my Granny's ground on two fields and a paddock for the horses. How well off we were in lots of ways, I thought to myself. I realised also that until that afternoon I had never told anyone outright that I was a Gypsy, until they had taken me at face value first. I was well on my way to retiring now, after working for twenty-one years for Social Services as a home help. I was born a Romany and yet I have never met a *gadje* (a non-Gypsy) that I would have changed places with. Looking back on my childhood is almost like looking through a golden bubble. All sorts of memories surface and appear at different times, almost as a beautiful dream, and yet it was real life for me. We saw each other every day, not just my parents and my brothers Teddy, Nelson and Christopher, my many cousins and young aunts and uncles, but most of all Granny and Granfer. Our days living on Granny's 'bit o' ground' were busy. We were surrounded by sweet-smelling bushes and trees, and heavily scented roses – pink and white – hanging heavy on the briars. So lovely to remember.

When we were children every day was an adventure. Summers seemed to last for ever and we got brown and healthy. Most of our days were spent doing exactly as we pleased. We had to do our chores first but then we were free to roam.

Our first thoughts were 'what shall we do today?' Whatever it was, no money was involved. We might go down to the river if the day was warm enough, paddling in the shallow water, or give my dog Tiny her weekly bath, which she enjoyed as much as we did. She was always reluctant to be coaxed out of the water, showering us all when she shook herself dry. We were very careful to keep away from sheep or any other livestock. Tiny was very good and had been taught not to chase animals of any kind. If any other dogs tried to involve her in a fight, she would sit quite still, gazing into the distance and ignoring them completely. She had a very gentle nature.

Or maybe Granny would come with us and we would pick plants and herbs for her to dry. In season we would collect all sorts of fruit. We knew where a wonderful wild damson tree grew. For years my cousins had kept this tree secret so that it would not be stripped of its fruit by anyone else. The fruit was sweet and delicious and as large as a plum. My mother loved them and so did Granny, so the fruits had to be carefully divided between them. Mum used to make a wonderful batter pudding with this lovely fruit. First she made a rich batter with full-fat milk, new-laid eggs and self-raising flour, and then she poured it into a baking dish, which had been heating in the oven with a large lump of lard in it. Then she added a large handful of stoned damsons. Forty-five minutes later our mouths were watering. At last Mum would take the pudding out of the oven and sprinkle it with sugar. We would eat it piping hot with custard. All was silence and not a scrap was left on our plates.

'That was lovely Mammy!' said my brothers.

'I wish I could eat that all over again,' I added. 'What a lovely treat!'

'What did yer Mammy do with they damsons?' Granny asked me. 'Did she stew 'em up?'

'Oh no, Granny, she made such a lovely pudding. Even Daddy had a bit! He said he wished there were a bit more!'

'What?' said Granny, ''ow could she make they damsons into a pudden?' Granny was not a good cook by any stretch of the imagination. She fed her family well but her ideas of how to put good food together were sadly lacking and unusual. Nevertheless I told her the recipe and so Granny set to and made her pudden. First she shooed us all out so she could concentrate. We all hovered around hoping for another piece of pie. When it was cooked and smelling heavenly, she took it out of the oven. It was all puffed up and golden brown. Granny looked as puffed up as her lovely pudden. As she picked up a large spoon, the pudding completely deflated. She tried to put a little on a saucer but it was just a curdled mess.

'Oh dear! What's wrong?' we gasped.

Granny spooned some more onto saucers. 'Nothin's wrong.'

We tried to eat it.

'The damsons taste lovely Granny,' I said quietly.

'What? It's just like yer Mammy's!' We did not reply. It was nothing like my mother's. I told my mother later how Granny's pudding had been spoilt but we didn't know how. The next time my mother made her damson batter pudding, I took mine to show Granny.

'Well, well! I don't know where I be goin' wrong but yer Mammy's looks right and mine don't.'

I told my mother what Granny had said. Mammy looked a bit worried.

'I'll ask her what she's putting in her pudding but she hates to be told.'

However, Mammy took her courage in both hands and in a very careful way she asked what ingredients Granny had put in her recipe. Granny gave her the list.

'Oh,' said Mammy, 'you did exactly right. The only thing that's missing is ... you left out the flour.'

Granny looked straight at me. 'You bad gal, Rosie. You told me wrong. It's your fault! I knowed mine would be better than yer Mammy's!'

'Don't blame Rosie. She only tried to help you. She only forgot one ingredient,' said Mammy.

'Yes, I know that now,' said Granny, 'but that's the most important one of all!' She flung her pinny off in annoyance. My mother tried to soothe her.

'You make another. Just make sure the fat's very hot and so is the oven.'

'Don't tell me 'ow to cook gal. I wuz doin' it afore 'ee wuz born!'

'Right then. I'll just watch,' said Mammy. When Granny's second attempt came out of the oven, we all had a saucer full, including Granfer and my father.

'That was lovely, Granny,' we all said truthfully.

'I told 'ee I could do better than yer Mammy!' she told us, looking extremely pleased with herself.

'You forgot the sugar on top though,' said my youngest brother Chris.

'I didn't see thee leavin' any,' said Granny, pinching his cheek not entirely kindly.

*

The winters were cold. The winter of 1947–1948 was particularly bitter. We could not keep warm easily. We were encouraged to keep moving and run around by our parents and teachers, to no avail. Our knees and lips were chapped. Mum put Vaseline on our lips and faces but we licked it off, which made matters worse and our lips bled. One fortunate little boy at my school came in one morning with a woolly jerkin and long corduroy trousers with lovely leather boots. We all envied him. He told us it was a present from an aunty in America. He was duly sent home with a note saying his clothing was not suitable for school wear. His parents took no notice and sent him to school in his lovely new clothes. He was probably the only child there who was warm that winter.

I only felt warm when we were sitting around Granny's range or making toast in front of our own. I remember my father coming home from the pub and feeling the sudden wonderful warmth as he threw his overcoat over my feet at the bottom of the bed. I could smell the odour of beer and cigarettes, a smell I cannot bear today, but it was so comforting back then that I would get warm and comfortable and soon drift back to sleep. Granfer would get up early, even in the winter, and light the campfire, placing the big black kettle on the kettle iron and making sure it nestled in the heart of the red-hot centre. It would quickly come to the boil and water would splutter out onto the fire, sending steam and ash into the air, threatening to put out the fire but never doing so. Sometimes if I was awake and dressed in time, I would call my brother Nelson to come with me and we would go and have a cup of tea with Granfer: strong dark tea with not much milk and plenty of sugar. I still like my tea strong and dark today. We would crouch down in front of the campfire to drink it, roasting at the front and freezing at the back.

'Stand back from the smoke!' Granfer would say, 'or 'ee will stink of it an' yer teacher will tell 'ee off!'

The teacher would often tell us off, asking if we had been sitting in a bonfire. We must have smelled strongly of smoke because even I could smell it in my hair when I combed it.

Sometimes if my brother Nelson was up early, Granfer would tell him to go and ask Mammy if he could go to the market with him. Nelson would run off as fast as his skinny legs could take him.

'Mammy! I's not goin' t' school t'day,' he would shout in excitement. It would have taken a much harder heart than my mother possessed to say no. My mother trusted Granfer to take care of Nelson. He was such a little boy and never very strong, but the fresh air and the occasional swig of cider seemed to do him good. At times he came back a little shaky on his feet but my mother would not have stopped him going with Granfer for anything. It would have broken his heart. He was dressed and ready to go hours before Granfer was ready to take him, and so Granfer would gently tease him.

'What be thee waitin' fer boy? Be thee goin' somewhere, eh?' he growled as he ruffled Nelson's spiky blond hair. Nelson knew Granfer was only teasing and he would never let him down. He had perfect trust in him. Granfer had taken us all on little trips from time to time. 'Voyages' he called them. My brother Teddy reminded me recently of all the trips he took with Granfer with Billy Pony and his cart.

'We only went a few miles,' he told me, 'but it seemed like the drive went on for ever! Now and then, on a quiet part o' the road, 'e would say to me, "Yer boy, 'ee take the reins fer a bit!" and I, afeared but overjoyed to be trusted, took the reins while Granfer kept 'is 'and ready, "just in case 'ee needs it boy!"' Sometimes he did need it as Billy Pony sensed the difference and stopped by the roadside for a crafty nibble.

''E was a great old man,' Teddy said sadly. 'I really loved 'im. You know, he couldn't have been very old. He just seemed old to us.'

I think that the days my brothers spent voyaging around the markets and villages with Granfer and his horse and cart must have been some of the happiest days of his life. They all kept him company at some time or other and nearly always came home with some useless treasure, which they would either take apart or examine in minute detail. Hours of pleasure were enjoyed sitting on a little wooden stool in front of Granny's range while Granfer combed his silver hair into a precise kiss curl, singing away to himself, his feet resting contentedly on the fire rail.

'My Edwin,' Granny would say, 'make room for yer cup o' Ovaltine and a bit o' toasted bread. I bought some good best butter in town.'

'Thank 'ee my dear Mary Ann. Don't 'ee ferget these boys. They bin workin' 'ard. They've 'elped I no end.'

'I won't ferget the boys,' Granny would say. She

would give them a mug each and a doorstep of toasted bread and butter. My brothers loved their food but it would take them ages to finish their toast. Finally Granfer would say, 'Hark! Boys, is that yer Mammy callin' fer 'ee? Time fer bed.'

Off they would go, tired out and full up. Granny often said she thought Granfer enjoyed those little trips more than the boys did. When the boys had gone, Granny and Granfer would take out the box of spectacles that Granfer had bought on his trips to the markets. Solemnly, they tried on every pair one by one, testing each other or just looking in the mirror to see if they suited them. My cousin Mary said she sat in the corner one evening watching them. She said that she laughed so much she had pains in her back and stomach for days. They tested each other with a newspaper, although neither of them could read, holding the paper far away and then closer. Granny even tried on her coat and hat to see which pair suited her best. Granfer was admiring himself, combing his kiss curl this way and that. It was better than the pictures, Mary said. The best bit, she said, was Granny rooting through the box until she came across something interesting.

'Well, well, my Edwin, well, well!'

'What is it, my Mary Ann?'

Standing up as tall as possible, she held up a pair of lorgnettes. Then turning her head haughtily she glared at Granfer through the eyepiece.

'Is the conveyance to hand, my good man?' she said.

'Oh Mary Ann! Don't thee go apin' the gentry!' Granfer responded.

Mary was still in hysterics as she recalled the scene.

'I even waked up laughin'!' What made it funnier was that Granfer was so carried away by the sight of his Mary Ann playin' the haughty lady, he almost believed it, but as soon as she put down the lorgnettes she was his dear Mary Ann again.

Granny never had much of a sense of humour. Life to her was very real and she worked very hard to make it a bit easier for all of us. Now and then her sense of the ridiculous surfaced and had us laughing for days. I think most of our family has a strong sense of the ridiculous. It has overcome me at the most inopportune times but I still would not be without it.

Granfer was a man of peace and to be with him was to feel it. He was much loved by us all, and my brother Nelson especially loved to listen to Granfer singing to himself as he whittled away at his wooden flowers. If Nelson picked up enough words, he would sing quietly to himself until he fell asleep: 'Little Dolly Daydream, Pride of I dunno ...' over and over, which had us all in fits as the words were 'Pride of Idaho'. We tried correcting him, but he preferred his own version.

Of us cousins there were almost too many to list. There was Violet, who was misnamed (she was more like an exotic poppy), our Chris, who was spoilt by all of us, my cousin Johnny, who was always peeping in birds' nests and peering down rabbit holes, trying to coax the baby rabbits out, our Teddy, the sensible one, and me. Carol, Henry, Valerie and Betsy would join us and we would spend whole days running through the fields and abandoned orchards eating our fill of the ripe fruit hanging untouched from the gnarled branches.

My cousin Johnny had dogs, cats and all sorts of birds but nothing was kept in cages. He loved his animals and was forever talking about them and what they could do. He was extremely patient with them and never harmed these defenceless creatures. When he showed us his newborn foals, he called them 'the most beautiful creatures in the whole world'. I believed that he was right but then I would see a tiny kitten, a puppy, or one of Uncle Fred's little pink piglets, and then I would think that each one of them was the most beautiful of all; and what could possibly be more delightful than a day-old chick with its fluffy yellow down, cheeping away with dozens of its brothers and sisters? We were so blessed to have all these wonders to see and touch. Nature programmes on the television are all very well but watching the birth of a puppy on a screen can never compare with feeling the warmth of a new puppy cuddled up in your arms and the tickle of it as it puts out its tiny pink tongue and licks your nose. Of course we took it all for granted. It is only in retrospect that we remember the joy it brought. We thought that every child enjoyed the same things we did.

Sometimes I would talk at school about my lovely dog, Tiny. When I told my classmates that she had had six puppies and that my daddy said they were all mine, they looked at me disbelievingly. I added, 'And Uncle Fred let me 'old the baby piglets last night. After their dinner they had apple pie and custard for their pudding!' At seeing the disbelief I would grab my cousin Bet's arm.

'It's true ain't it, Bet? Your dad gives his pigs pudding, don't he?'

Bet, knowing more than I did, would agree. 'Sometimes 'e gives 'em rhubarb and custard!'

'See!' I would insist, 'Bet's dad is my Uncle Fred and she should know what their pigs eat!'

I always felt safe with my faithful little dog. If anyone came into our yard and was what I considered a little too friendly to me (ruffling my hair for example), Tiny would sit in front of me, growling at the back of her throat to warn the perceived intruder to get back. Dad thought Tiny was to be praised for this and although he laughed he would say, 'Better step back old man! Anyone who looks sideways at our Rosie is liable to lose a few fingers just fer a start!' My Uncle Leonard was there one day when this happened. He had lost a few fingers from his left hand because he had not pulled his hands away from the circular saw in time. The visitor who had ruffled my hair did not know this and when Uncle Leonard thrust out his hand at the right moment, the man looked shocked and moved back slowly.

'I was only funning! I'm sorry little gel!' he apologised.

'I knows that,' said Dad, trying not to catch Uncle Leonard's eye, 'but it's best to be safe. I got that little dog fer our Rosie cause she was born on the same day as Rosie and Tiny has looked after her ever since.'

'Well,' said the man nervously, 'she certainly does a good job!'

My father laughed when he recounted what had happened to my mother that evening.

'Well she's a wonderful little dog,' Mum agreed.

'Have you ever noticed how she always sits with her eyes glued to Rosie and if anyone makes a sudden move she fixes her eyes on them until they calm down?' Mum was not mad on dogs, but her one exception was Tiny. We all loved her. I know that she loved and trusted me as I loved and trusted her.

Johnny loved Granfer's horse, Billy Pony, and although he was a carthorse, Johnny could not resist trying to mount him. Poor old Billy was only used to Granfer harnessing him to his lovely red and silver cart. Billy Pony put up with Johnny's escapades until one day he had had enough. Letting out a loud whinny, he turned his head, grabbed Johnny by the seat of his pants, turned and dropped him straight into the ditch.

'Uncle Eddy!' he shouted. 'Save me!'

My father did. All that was harmed was Johnny's dignity. How sorry and ashamed Johnny was. His father then realised that Johnny must have a pony of his own. He called her 'Sugar', which suited her very well. He was not selfish with her and he shared her with all of us. If we wanted a ride we could have one. He rode bareback and so did we. Sugar would take us up and down the field at a gentle trot, but that did not suit Johnny. His naughty streak would come to the surface and when we were seated he would smack Sugar on the rump and off we would go at a gallop. Well, a canter, but it felt like a gallop to us. I would have loved it if we had remained seated but often I would come off. I wonder now that I was not hurt. When Sugar came to a stop or I fell off in the mud, Johnny would rush up.

'You rode her well, Rosie!' he would say, a big smile all over his face. 'Well done!'

I would feel so pleased that I had done so well that I never complained about his naughty behaviour. I should have told my father that Johnny had made the horse gallop and I had fallen off in the mud, while he got off scot-free, but there was never any malice intended with Johnny. He loved a good gallop so he thought everyone else would. We did too, while we stayed on the horse.

My father used to be quite good about Johnny's pigeons. They used to plunder the peas and beans but when my father had a go at Johnny one day, Johnny, instead of getting upset, went and got his beautiful gold and white pigeon. He had only had it for a few days. His face shone as he tenderly stroked its feathers, just like a young father showing off his new baby.

'Yer've wasted yer bit o' vonger, Johnny,' he warned. 'The farmers 'll get 'im even if I don't!'

'You don't ever 'urt my birds Uncle Eddy,' he smiled, 'I seed you. You shoots to miss, yes you do!'

'Johnny, have yer ever seen a pigeon's crop when it's 'ad a good feed of my peas?'

'Yes,' said Johnny, 'I have. An' ain't it grand how they gets all that grub in that little pouch?'

'Yeh,' said Dad dryly, 'Ain't it grand.'

Needless to say my father's threats, unlike the pigeon's crop, were empty. He could not shoot Johnny's pigeons or anything else that moved except rats. That would not have worried Dad. They were filthy vermin and caused much damage. Johnny's heart would have been broken if anyone he knew tried to hurt any of his animals. He himself changed from a boisterous little boy who rushed here and there into a gentle lamblike boy stroking feathers and fur. He crooned to each creature until they completely relaxed in his grubby little-boy hands and fell asleep. He was such a mixture. He teased me often but was never cruel. His father bought him a cockerel: a magnificent bird with dark red feathers, a light red comb and a crow that could be heard for miles around. Johnny caught up with me after school.

'Come 'ome wi' me, Rosie, and I'll show you me cockerel eggs.'

I looked at him in disbelief and yet not quite sure. I knew what a tease he could be. I was only five and too inexperienced to be fully confident of my own common sense, yet I spoke up.

'No, Johnny. Cock birds can't lay eggs,' I said firmly, 'I know 'cause my Dad c'llects 'em from the hens.'

'Yes, I know that Rosie. You've got egg-layin' hens an' I got both. Me dad says cockerel's eggs are bigger than hens an' they only lay once a week an' then they lays two at a time. If it's the right time they has twins.' He seemed very self-assured. 'I was there once an' I seed it fer meself!'

I was in a whirl. I knew in my heart that the story he was telling me was not true. I had always known that chickens laid eggs, but if cockerels could not lay eggs, what use could they possibly be? I had heard Dad say that they were noisy and only good for a roast dinner, so was Johnny lying, or not? Johnny looked at me innocently: huge brown eyes, rosy cheeks and rumpled curly hair. I have to say I really liked Johnny, everyone did. He had a lovely nature and he always had something very funny to say.

'I'm going to ask my Mammy,' I decided.

'Your mammy won't know. She only knows about proper babies. Your Dad knows I 'specs.'

I followed him into his shed where he kept all of his little animals and birds. It was warm and smelled clean. Every creature was cared for and kept in suitable conditions. His current pet jackdaw, Jack, flew in the door and perched on his shoulder, pecking his ear and ruffling his hair. He hand-fed him with some grain and pointed to a huge cage.

'He's only fer tonight. Me Dad's puttin' him in with the chickens tomorrow. He laid two such gurt big eggs that one got stuck and me Dad had to get the vet to pull it out. We had they eggs fer our breakfast. Me mam scrambled 'em. There was enough fer five people!'

I gazed in awe at this amazing bird. He did seem to have a knowing look in his eye but I was not convinced.

'But Johnny, my dad told me that cock birds are the daddy birds and it's only mammies that can have babies. They've got a special little cradle thing in their bellies to put the babies. Daddy birds haven't got that. They just fight with the other daddy birds.'

For a minute Johnny seemed foxed. He went quiet.

'Have you told me lies Johnny?'

'I told the trufe,' he insisted. 'Your dad don't want you to know about my wonderful bird in case you wants one. I don't fink Uncle Eddy can afford a big bird like mine. I know he ain't as rich as my dad but you can share mine if you likes. I don't fink he'll lay any more eggs though. The vet had a real job getting the last one out.'

'Oh, Johnny,' I sighed. I think he would have made a wonderful storyteller. He could write stories by the dozen and we would all believe them because we wanted to. He did have more than we did, it is true, but he was kind and generous and shared everything. He used to tell us that one day he would have a farm of his own and would describe it to us until it was almost real. As it would prove to be: in later life he grew lots of vegetables that he would pick late in the day or early morning and pack them on his cart. He would collect eggs from his chickens and flowers from his garden. As far as I know he never sold any cockerel eggs, certainly never any twin ones.

Back in our childhood days, when we were out in the fields we kept an eye open for anything good and edible that we could take home to our parents. This was second nature to us all. You could say that although we were children, we thought as adults. Our parents were always pleased with our gleanings. Our days were spent doing things that made us look forward to our meals, however plain they might be, and at bedtime we would be ready for sleep and looking forward to the next day.

Through the golden bubble I recall the hours spent in the fields, running home down the lane in the warm summer dusk. No one looked for us if we were a bit late. Our parents knew we all kept together and looked after each other. Gadje ways and Romany ways are not that different in that respect, except perhaps Gypsy ways are more laid back. What happens will happen. Tomorrow is another day and things will go on much the same. Whenever I think of my childhood it seems full of music and laughter. It may have been hard at times, and I remember those occasions well, but then the gadjes had hard times too. Our hard times did not leave us with tight lips, frowns and a general air of misery, though. It was laughed off. It would not last and the good times would come again, so why worry?

We must have looked quaint, five or six of us all trailing home in the dusk singing our childish songs, collapsing into giggles or breaking into little runs, regrouping and making sure everyone was there and safe. Without fail, all of the girls and some of the boys held a posy of wild flowers for their mothers. These were received with a 'thank you my dove' or 'my little bird' or 'my flower'. We smiled with pleasure that our Mammies had liked our posies. We were well pleased.

2

Shepherd's Purse

My Granny and Granfer are never far from my mind. Granfer was Granny's 'my Edwin' and she was his dear 'Mary Ann'. They had chosen to live life the way they did and accepted financial hardship in exchange for the ultimate freedom to be true to themselves. When I was very young indeed, I recall three posh shiny black cars drawing into our yard at the camp. Three handsome young men in suits had stepped out. Many years later, I mentioned this to my mother and asked her if she knew who they were.

'Goodness me! You were only three years old then. Those posh cars were Cadillacs and they belonged to the young men.'

'Was one of them Granfer?' I asked.

'No, one of them was his younger brother and the other two were his older brothers. They were very wealthy men. They had done very well for themselves in business and they wanted Granfer to come in with them. It was a very successful business they had set up.'

'Was it just Granfer they wanted?'

'Yes, just Granfer.'

'Well, I'm glad he didn't go.'

'So was Granny!' laughed Mum.

'I might have been very young but I remember Granfer shouting and I have never heard Granfer shout at any other time in my life. He never lost his temper. I remember him shouting, "Be gone thy son of a ring-tailed monkey!"'

Mum stared at me. 'Fancy you remembering that!'

'Well, Mum, those words were so wonderful. I had never heard anyone use that phrase before or since and to hear my dear Granfer saying that in such a rage was unforgettable.'

'Well, you obviously didn't forget. I remember it well too.'

'What was it all about, Mum?' I asked. I was old enough to be told by then.

'Well, even I don't know for sure, but I think they had done very well in dealing in gold. They wanted Granfer to give up his Gypsy life and go in with them. The offer was just for him, no one else. Not even his dear Mary Ann. Not even the clothes he had on. He was to become a different person and lead a totally different way of life.'

'But why?' I asked.

'Who knows?'

'Well I'm very glad he didn't go,' I said.

How different our lives would have been without our beloved Granfer. He loved the life he led. He had many friends from all walks of life and the love of his large family. He dealt with the upper classes, buying and selling horses. He had enough money for his needs and he had his freedom. He was not tied to the clock nor did he bow his head to any man. I am not at all surprised that he lost his temper with the men who tried to take all this away from him. I think perhaps that 'son of a ring-tailed monkey' was a bit too kind for them. Granfer was a king to us. What did gold mean to him? He had his sovereign on his watch chain and a gold ring with rubies. That was enough for him.

'I don't want t' worry 'bout gold and jewellery,' he used to say, 'there's allus bad people who want t' take it off 'ee. A peaceful life is all I wants.'

Granny and Granfer were part of the earth they lived on and lived life accordingly. It was a hard life in some ways and even harder for my mother, yet she never complained. It would have helped if my mother had been allowed to go out to work, but my father said no and there was no arguing. The only exception was at Christmas time when he allowed her to go out with my aunts selling holly and mistletoe cut from the local hedgerows and trees. That was only because the money was needed for extra food and maybe a small gift for the younger children. Money was short and not to be spent on cheap toys that would not last five minutes. Back then not a penny was wasted.

When I was a small child of five or six, clothing was bought with coupons. My mother made my little frocks from remnants of gingham. A yard of material was sixpence and this would make two little dresses for me. Her own clothes lasted her for years. By adding a brooch or a little bit of lace she would make them look fresh and new. She would sell a few of her clothing coupons so that she could afford something else she needed. Mum sewed everything by hand in those days, although later on Granny acquired an old Singer sewing machine, which she borrowed. I remember a dark grey, swing back jacket that she made from a pure wool blanket. It had a wide collar and turned-back cuffs. She wore what I thought was a diamond brooch pinned to the reveres. Even to my childish eyes she looked really pretty. When my father saw her coat, he could not believe it was made from a woollen blanket. Mum had to show him what was left of it. He thought Mum could do anything. We did as well. The only one who was not impressed was Granny.

'Fancy makin' a coat, Mary, when 'ee needs beddin'.'

'We've got enough blankets. I really needed a coat,' said Mum. 'Get me another blanket and I'll make you one.'

Granny tut-tutted some more until Granfer butted in.

'Mary Ann, don't 'ee begrudge the gal a coat. Thee's got a lovely warm coat. I seen Mary's old coat. She's had'n fer years. She looked right shabby in it!' Then, looking my father in the eye, he said, 'I'm surprised 'ee ain't noticed it our Eddy!'

My father, like most men, never noticed anything unless it was under his nose. 'I think my Mary looks lovely,' he said, 'an' real clever!'

Mum wore the coat for years. In the end she bought one from a shop but she could never bring herself to throw the other one away, so the moths put paid to it.

'Never mind, there's still enough to make your little brother a pair of trousers,' she said, looking on the bright side of things. It was very difficult to buy all the things a family needs, so the women in those days had to be extremely resourceful.

I often wished that I was as good at sewing as my mother, but even sewing on a button was beyond me. A needle would turn into a dangerous weapon in my hand, the pristine piece of material into a grubby piece of rag instead of the delightful tray cloth that all my school friends had presented to our beaming teacher. No beaming smile for me, just a sad frown and the usual question:

'What on *earth* is *this*?' Followed by, 'How is it possible for the other little girls to turn in beautiful hand work and *you*,' she would say emphatically, 'present me with something that closely resembles a *used* dish cloth?' This was stated more in sorrow than in anger. I remember it well.

'I don't know, Miss,' I would reply, hanging my head with shame.

'Just go and sit down. Take it home. Perhaps your mother will wash it for you.'

Well, my mother did wash it for me but it still looked a mess. The teacher held it up and sighed.

'If you think I'm going to pay one and sixpence for that, I'm afraid you're much mistaken!'

Somewhere between school and home it 'got lost'. Nothing was said about it and I, for one, was very glad.

Needlework was not a gift I had been bestowed with,

so how could I possibly win first prize in a needlework competition? We had all been given the assignment of sewing a patch and had each been given an identical square of cloth with a small hole in and another piece to patch it with. The aim was to sew it in place with invisible stitches. The first prize was seven shillings and sixpence, a lot of money for a child of ten back then. I had no illusions of winning. In fact, I thought it a complete waste of time, but I did my best, handed it in with the others and forgot all about it.

A week later, during the half term, a flower show was held locally. I did not go. On returning to school, the first thing we did was collect all the baby frogs that were hopping around the classroom. Then after Morning Prayer and a song, I was called to the front. My first thought was that I must have done something wrong, but my class teacher was beaming broadly and holding out her hand to me. I stood next to her and my needlework teacher as they presented me with first prize in the sewing class. I could not believe it. I just stood there in shock staring at the postal order I had been given and the piece of needlework that my teacher held aloft for all to admire.

'Yes, you may well look shocked, Rosemary,' she said through a clenched smile as everyone clapped, 'but you are not as shocked as I am!'

I stared hard at the patched cloth. I was sure it could not be mine. But whose was it?

'Miss,' I whispered, 'I don't think this is my sewing!'

'It was in your workbox with your name pinned to it. Who would prefer *your* work to their own?'

All day long I pondered over that question. Whose delicate stitches had been in my workbox? When I ran home to tell my mother she could not believe it either.

'Never!' she said incredulously, holding the piece of work and checking the postal order with my name on it.

'Well you can either spend it or return it. It's up to you!'

Being very young and seeing as the teacher had not argued with me, I spent it. My conscience still pricked me though, so the next time I saw my needlework teacher I reaffirmed my suspicions.

'I'm sure that sewing wasn't mine, Miss,' I said.

'Have you spent the prize money?' she asked with a steely glare.

'Yes, Miss.'

'Well then, unless you can pay it back I would advise you to keep quiet!'

So that was that. Except, more than twenty years later, my mother gave me a box of bits and pieces that she thought my eldest two daughters would like. Going through it, I found a little parcel of tissue paper. There was the beautifully sewn patch, wrapped in delicate tissue and still spotlessly clean. Seeing it again after so many years, I could safely say to myself, 'This ain't my sewing, Miss!' I grieved for the small girl whose work it really was and who had been deprived of her rightful prize. I wonder if there is someone, somewhere who remembers a grotty piece of sewing, knowing full well it was not hers?

*

As a small child being brought up on Granny's 'bit o' ground' I really had no idea of how people with 'nice houses' or enough money lived. The lives of the people in the storybooks I read were pure fantasy and did not bear any resemblance to the life I knew. Looking back down the years I realise that our lives were hard and many things we regarded as luxuries were commonplace to many gadjes. On the other hand there were many children I went to school with who were just as poor as we were. Simple things such as peeling an orange take me back to my classroom and my teacher telling us to get ready for P.E. It was a really bitter day. Even she realised how cold it would be for us running around outside in our vests and knickers.

'We will do our arithmetic first,' she said. 'It will be a little warmer in an hour or so.' That was wishful thinking, as it never did get any warmer. 'First of all we will talk about what we did at the weekend.'

That was hardly worthwhile. Most of us had just tried to keep warm. One little girl, who was poorer than most, held up a beautiful orange. Most children had never seen, let alone tasted, an orange so we were all enthralled.

'I'll give my best friends the peel but I've got to eat my orange. My mummy said.'

We knew we would not be getting any, so we had to be content just to admire it.

'Put it on your desk and we will get ready for P.E.,' came the teacher's voice.

A class of thirty or so skinny children reluctantly undressed for P.E. It was years before I realised what

P.E. actually stood for, but I knew exactly what it meant. Out we ran into the bitterly cold day in our vests and knickers, hugging our shoulders in an effort to keep warm.

'Run around! Run around! That will warm you up!' There she stood, fully clothed in coat, boots, hat, scarf and gloves while we tried our best to keep our circulation going in our skimpy underwear. Blue with the cold, our teeth banging together, we were told by her to march into school. When I think of this cruel behaviour, I am appalled. Finally, we were shepherded into the relative warmth of the classroom. We were all trying to get dressed – no easy task with numb fingers – when a piercing shriek rang out.

'Me orange! Me orange has gone!'

We all turned in shock at the empty space where the orange had been. No orange. Where could it be? There was only one door to the classroom and we had seen no one enter or leave.

'Look in your desk, silly girl!'

Still no orange. More screams. We all joined in the search, looking high and low. Finally we gave up. The former owner of the orange sat and sobbed heartbrokenly.

'I was lookin' forward to me orange,' she sniffled into her sleeve. The teacher was irritated.

'Well it's not here. Be quiet and get on with your lesson.'

'It *was* yer though,' piped up my cousin Johnny, 'and now it ain't. So where's it gone?'

'That's none of your concern, John.'

Johnny continued undeterred. 'If it wuz yourn, an' it wuz took, you might cry as well.'

'Be quiet boy and get your books out!'

Johnny would not be stopped. 'It wuz a 'uge mouse, Miss. I did see it once when I wuz kept in an' it wuz quiet.'

'It's never quiet when you are around John. You are a very noisy boy.'

'Yes, Miss. I wuz very quiet cuz I wuz eating me bar o' choclit that Rosie's dad give me fer cleanin' out the ferrets – didn't 'e Rosie?' he said, looking straight at me. I said nothing. It was probably true. Dad always gave his sweet ration to us children. He never had much money so he bribed or rewarded us all with chocolate. Johnny continued. There was no stopping him; I knew that only too well. He continued weaving his web around us all, entrancing us with his story. Even the little girl with the orange stopped sniffing.

'I wuz very quiet, eatin' away when sudden like, out popped a little twitchin' nose. "Johnny," I says to meself, "that be a mouse!" I looked an' stayed lookin' an' 'e did come out a bit more. I could see 'is little whiskers all a twitchin'.' Then, turning to the teacher, who was as mesmerised as we were, he said, 'Right where yer foot is, Miss!'

With a shriek she lifted her foot off the floor, while the whole class fell about laughing. 'Silly boy! Be quiet!'

But Johnny was determined to finish his tale.

'I knowed 'e wanted me choclit, so what did I do? I left 'alf a bar in me desk. I thought it'd be clever if 'e got in me desk an' took that there bit o' choclit! Next day

30

I lifted up the lid an' me choclit wuz gone! Not even a crumb. I could see where 'e had been though cuz he'd weed hisself, so I did know.'

'You disgusting boy!' hissed the teacher. 'If that is remotely true, I hope you cleaned up the mess!'

'No, it soon dried up.'

'What has this nonsense got to do with a lost orange?'

'Well Miss, I wuz just gettin' to that. Me dad says if yer see one mouse, there's 'undreds yer don't see. One little mouse might not get 'er orange into that there 'ole but if they all 'ad a bit, it wouldn't take long would it Miss?'

Our teacher could not speak for a moment; she just gazed at Johnny silently.

'You foolish, foolish boy,' she gasped, 'I've never heard such rubbish!'

Johnny said nothing, but, turning and catching my eye, he gave me a huge wink and a smile. I, for one, would rather listen to Johnny's stories – which often held an element of truth – than do my arithmetic. The precious orange was never found but I have never remembered that day without also thinking of the mouse who managed to get a huge orange into a tiny mouse hole. I may have taken Johnny's stories with a pinch of salt, but only a tiny pinch because in my heart I always wanted them to be true.

When I was a very small child the roads were very quiet except for the Gypsy wagons we frequently saw, maybe five or six wagons with their dogs, horses and large families. They often had babies: lovely little beings, loved and cherished by their families and dressed in the best they could afford. Sometimes they had asked householders if they had any little clothes for them. My own Granny often brought home things for our babies and these in turn were passed around the family. Times were very hard in the thirties and forties. Most people found it difficult to survive, not just us but gadjes as well. Many men had no jobs and tramped the roads. Tramps frequently stopped at our camp: men who had fought in a dreadful war and lost a leg, arm or an eye. Often their homes had gone and their families had been killed in the Blitz or just disappeared. Granny rarely turned them away no matter how little she had. She always gave them a cup of tea and some food. It wasn't in her to refuse. Young as we were, we learned a valuable lesson from this. One or two of these men stayed for several weeks, helping to plant our few crops and doing odd jobs. Somehow they always seemed more at peace with themselves when they finally left our camp.

My cousin Britt rang me up recently and reminded me of an incident that had happened when one of these men had visited. He had stayed for a while and on the morning he left, my mother was doing her weekly wash. As usual, she took off her rings and put them in a small dish on the top step of the wagon and pushed it back into the corner. When she had finished her laundry and went to fetch her rings, they had gone. Mum thought she had made a mistake or they had fallen off the step. She looked everywhere. The dish was still there but the rings had completely disappeared. Finally she sat down and cried. I helped her to look and tried to comfort her.

'Oh Mammy, don't worry. Daddy will buy you some more.'

'No, Rosie,' she sighed, 'Daddy won't have enough money to buy any more. They cost a lot of money. What *shall* I do?'

When Dad heard about the loss he was really angry.

'Why didn't you keep 'em on?'

My mother just shook her head silently. Ironically, she had taken them off for safety as my Aunt Prissy had once lost a ring while rinsing her washing over the runaway that ran into the ditch.

'Have that tramp bin yer?' Dad asked suspiciously.

'He went early. I still had them on then.'

Well, it was a mystery. Mum could not rest. Dad could not be angry for long. He could see how broken-hearted Mum was over the loss of her wedding ring. I kept looking around the outside of the wagon but it was a waste of time.

A few days later, my cousin Johnny wandered into the yard. His father was with him. He wanted to see my parents.

'Uncle Eddy,' Johnny began, 'Yer knows my jackdaw, Jack?'

'Yes, I do remember.'

'Well, yer knows when I brought 'im down to show your Rosie the little tricks that I learned 'im?'

'Yes, I did see.'

'Well 'e picks up all these pretty things in 'is beak an'

'e flies away an' 'ides 'em in 'is nest box up 'ome in the shed.'

'Yes,' said Dad, light beginning to dawn.

'Well, 'old out yer 'and Aunty Mary,' he commanded.

Mum, looking a bit bewildered, held out her hand and, with a triumphant smile, Johnny dropped Mum's rings and a gold brooch into her outstretched hand. She could not believe her eyes.

'Oh thank you, Johnny! *Thank* you!'

'Don't be too thankful,' said Dad dryly, 'it was '*is* fault they was lost in the first place!'

'The brooch isn't mine though,' said Mum.

'You keep it,' smiled Johnny. 'If I 'ear about some-buddy losin' a brooch yer can give it me back.'

I wear my mother's wedding ring on my finger. It is a lovely ring and I value it now and always. What happened to the little brooch I do not know.

Uncle Alfie lost a ring, too, when I was about eleven. He was planting peas and beans in Granny's field. The peas were a bush variety that only grow about ten or twelve inches high. Uncle Alfie had spent most of the day planting. It was only when he was washing his hands under the standpipe that he noticed that his ring was missing. We all knew how Uncle Alfie valued that ring, not because it was worth a lot of money but because the only girl he had ever loved gave it to him. It was a wide gold ring with two snakes' heads entwined with rubies for eyes. Uncle Alfie was a quiet man and did not make too much fuss but asked us all to look out for it when we could. All the children searched and searched but we felt the ring was lost for ever.

'Thanks fer lookin' anyway,' he said sadly, 'but I knows it's gone.'

Granny offered him one of her rings.

'This be a man's ring our Alfie. See if it fits 'ee.'

'No, it's not the same,' he said.

We children did not know the whole story but we knew the ring had a great deal of sentimental value. Time passed, summer came and went and everyone helped to harvest the vegetables.

'Pea pickin' in the mornin'!' we were all told. Those of us who were able to pick did so. The day was hot for September.

'Uncle Alfie, if the ice-cream man comes, will you buy us an ice cream?' we begged.

'Yes,' he said and laughed. 'Keep an eye on Tiny. That dog always knows when the van's comin'!'

We began picking, chatting and laughing as we picked.

'I hope we have some of these peas for our supper,' I said to Violet.

'You've already ate your share!' joked Alfie, 'it's one in the basket and two in yer mouth!'

It was true. I loved the baby peas straight from the pod but I did try not to eat any more. We were nearing the end of the row when one of the boys suddenly shouted.

'Uncle Alfie! Come quick!'

We all rushed over to see what the excitement was about.

'Look Uncle!' he pointed. 'Jest look, don't touch it!'

Uncle Alfie followed his finger, as did the rest of us.

'Oh my dear! Look at that!' Alfie gasped in wonderment. There was Uncle Alfie's precious ring! The pea stalk had grown right through the centre of the ring and there it hung looking just like a flower. Uncle Alfie's sailor-blue eyes sparkled with tears of joy.

'Thank 'ee!' he said pushing it back on his finger. 'Thank 'ee!'

We were all so happy for him. Then, just as if it was meant to be, Tiny started barking.

'You lot wait by the gate, the ice-cream van'll be yer soon,' said Uncle Alfie. He bought us all a double ice cream and a cone for Tiny. We all enjoyed our treat but no one could have been happier than our dear Uncle Alfie. He could not stop looking at his lovely ring and exclaiming about the magical way it had been found. We had so few possessions that whatever we owned was all the more precious to us.

The fairs, visiting wagons, new faces and the fruit-picking season all made our daily lives varied and more interesting. There was always something to look forward to. One travelling Gypsy family stayed with us on Granny's land for about three weeks. They had three small girls: two aged about three or four and a baby of a few months. The mother of the family was always trying to get through her day without a mishap. She never seemed to be able to finish one job before starting another. You may think that having just a vardoe and a lean-to tent to live in, would have made life fairly easy.

Nothing she had was ever put away and she could never find anything.

'Can you 'elp me, Betty?' she asked my cousin, who lived with Aunt Betsy.

'How?' asked Betty, looking dubious.

'Take the babby fer a bit, and Patience and Priscilla. I'll pay yer.'

Betty reluctantly agreed. From then on she looked after the children almost full-time for their mother. She took advantage and left them with Betty longer and longer. Poor Betty was worn out. She was only seventeen or so. No payment was forthcoming and Betty did not know how to ask for it. The children's mother was off to town on the bus or else hawking her basket around wealthy homes. When my mother saw Betty looking somewhat frazzled she asked her what was going on. Betty cried she was so tired. Mum promised to help her. When the mother arrived back from hawking she showed Mum her haul.

'Look yer Mary. Ain' this pretty?'

She held up what were obviously new sets of satin underwear.

'I asked this young woman if she could ' elp me and she gives me this pile of clothes that she were going to give 'er friend. She said, "Take this an' go!" so I did! I think she made a mistake giving me this lot.'

Mum could see the quality was first-class.

'What are you going to do with these? They're too small for you!'

'Oh, I can get a lot for they pretty things,' she replied airily.

Mum picked them up. Pink, blue and cream petticoats and French knickers with heavy lace frilled around the hems. She looked the young mother straight in the eye.

'Betty's looked after your children for three weeks. Three sets of undies, that's one set a week. It hardly covers it but it'll do.'

'No!' she cried, trying to snatch back the undies, but Mum was quicker.

'Come and fetch your children then and pay Betty what you owe her or else give her these,' said Mum firmly.

'I was gonna give 'er ten bob.'

'What – ten bob a week?' asked Mum.

'No, of course not. Ten bob fer the three weeks.'

'I don't think so,' said Mum. 'She's given them their meals as well.'

She went and fetched the children and gave Betty the new underwear.

'You should have seen Betty's face,' said Mum at suppertime. 'Just her size as well. She just keeps looking at them.'

'I'll be glad to see that lot go,' said Dad. 'They be nothin' but trouble!'

'Well Rosie,' said Mum, 'what do you think?'

'I be glad Mammy.'

'Why are you glad?' she asked, laughing.

'Well, do you remember when Betty asked me to iron her pretty satin petticoat that Aunty Doreen gave her?'

'Yes I do. It was a bit silly of her to ask a five-year-old girl to do her ironing for her, I thought.'

My dear mother in her twenties

Granny in Town
on an outing
with her sister

Aunt Britt and Granny in Town. A cold day out
but still smiling!

Mum with *her* mum. Putting the world to rights
on a regular Saturday visit

Me playing at being a model, taken by Violet.
She has an identical one taken by me

Our Wedding Day, 1956

Showing off my ring. Were we ever that young?

Wedding group, except everyone is standing just anywhere!

Me and my cousin Violet. I was visiting my parents, age 19

'I remember. I put the hot iron right in the middle of her petticoat and when I lifted it up an iron-shaped piece of petticoat was stuck to the iron!'

I also remembered the sick feeling that came over me when I looked at Betty's face. Her eyes filled with tears and so did mine.

'I'm so sorry, Betty,' I had said.

'It's all right, Rosie, I shouldn't've asked yer to do it. Yer's only a little gal but you always seem so sensible.'

She was so gracious to me though and did not blame me for the mishap. I was glad she had three new sets now. She deserved it. Betty could not bear to hurt anyone's feelings. I have always remembered how kind she was. Betty was my Aunt Prissy's daughter and her sisters were Rosina, Mary and young Prissy. They all had lovely manners and Rosina had a wonderful personality. It was such a shame that they were left orphans at such a young age but they were all cared for by different members of the family. No one went into care while there was a community willing to look after them. Family mattered and it was good that they all lived close to each other and were able to see each other whenever they wanted to. They remained very close, loving sisters.

Although Romany life was often a struggle, it brought many joys and the benefits of living in a warm and caring community were more valuable than gold. When I was still very young, I knew that a Gypsy was born in his parents' bed and slept there until the next baby came along. When the time came, he would die in his own bed. They never worried that their families would put them in 'a home'. Unless there was a serious illness that could only be treated with nursing care, they helped each other until the end and never asked for anything in return.

3

Bindweed and Daisies

As a child, my life was lived in two distinct parts, which were completely separate in my view: school and home. That was the way I liked it. From the moment I started school I encountered prejudice and unwarranted disapproval from children and teachers alike. The children had learned it in ignorance from their parents, but the teachers who allowed it to continue without consequence were more responsible. It was shocking to me to be treated in such an unjust way when all I had ever known was the warm love and respect of my Romany family. False accusations and name-calling were almost daily occurrences for me and my cousins, but my dear Granfer taught me to hold my head up high and to know that I was as good as anyone.

A well remembered incident in my schooldays was when my Aunt Amy, Bet's mother, went and read the riot act to the bully of a headmaster at our school. After he had my cousin Bet on the carpet for some trivial misdemeanour, he caned her in front of the class, hard enough to bruise her hand. Bet was brave. She held back the tears and went back to her seat. Her hand was so painful afterwards she could not hold her pen, although she tried.

'Never mind, Bet,' we whispered, 'Yer Mam'll sort him out!'

Sure enough, at nine o'clock the next morning, in raged Bet's mother. She was only a little woman but she had a lot of courage. She faced the headmaster.

'Who gave you permission to cane my Bet?' she stormed, 'she never gets hit at 'ome. 'Er own father's never lifted a finger to our gals. We looks after 'em well. We don't need no interference from a man who 'its little gals!'

Her gaze swept the room.

'My children are looked after as well as any in this room!' And, poking her finger into his chest, she added, 'Don't you ever 'it my children again!'

'They have to be punished if they don't behave, Mrs Bailey,' he said, backing away.

'What did she do?' asked Aunt Amy.

'She clattered her chair after she and the class had been told to be quiet.'

'My dear man,' said Aunt Amy scornfully, 'I think you likes 'ittin' children. I 'eard you caned one of our little ones so bad 'is 'and was all swelled up an' 'im only five yers old! I think yer enjoys it!'

With that she grabbed Bet's hand and pulled her out of the class. As far as I know, Bet was never caned again and we never forgot Aunt Amy's utter rage. I do think that hitting children, especially if they are not your own, is so wrong. The punishment should fit the crime. Children remember that and learn from it.

There is a poem I was introduced to recently called 'Timothy Winters'. It is about a young lad who was unloved and uncared for. The poem goes on to describe how his clothes were in rags, he was barefoot and the wind blew through his clothes, yet when they were praying for the poor, his was the loudest voice of all. I find it very touching. There was a boy at school who accurately fitted the description of the boy in the poem. I remember him well.

Our teacher was holding auditions one day for the play *Treasure Island*. I was supposed to have the part of this boy's mother. I was not all that keen; I thought it was more of a boy thing. At fourteen, I hardly looked right for it. I looked at him in despair. He caught me looking at him and blushed to the roots of his red hair, his reddened complexion hiding for a brief moment his huge orange freckles. At once I felt sorry for him. He was always in trouble for something; being sent out to wash the tide mark off his neck or for wearing his ripped jumper back to front so as the big hole would not show through. The teacher humiliated him at every opportunity.

'You fool, boy!' he boomed at him, 'The folk behind you can still see the hole even if those in the front cannot!'

Poor boy. He grinned as though he did not care. Those of us who had also been shown up by this bully knew how he felt. He cared as deeply as we all did when we were shown up, but we just put up with it while we seethed silently with anger. The audition continued. None of us could act for toffee and we just wanted to get it over with and go home.

'No one will leave this room until this audition is over,' said the teacher.

Oh no. This was not fair. Many of the children had jobs to go to, and not just jobs to earn a little pocket money but money that was badly needed to put food on the table and to help with clothing.

'I've got a job, Sir. I must leave on time!' pleaded one boy.

'And me!' said another.

'I've got to look after our babby. Me mam's got a cleaning job and she'll be angry if I'm not home,' said one of the girls.

The teacher did not care about their personal lives and showed it with a sneer. Just then, an older boy spoke up, standing squarely in front of him, his face burning with rage.

'I don't care about your poxy play! Me dad don't neither. I have to help on our farm. He needs me 'cause me mam's dying. I got to be there for her and me dad!' So saying he turned on his heel and walked out. The teacher knew it would be better to give in against such mass dissent. It was the easier option.

'Be here same time tomorrow,' he sighed.

I admired anyone who had the courage to stand up for themselves. This was a huge part of our upbringing. Don't let anybody think you're afraid. Keep your head up. Don't let anybody get you down. I still believe in this.

We were all lined up for the audition the following day. What a rag, tag and bobtail lot we all looked. We would not have to worry about costumes; we all looked wrecks. After the problems the previous day, the audition was over quickly. I was not looking forward to the play. I knew the teasing I would get from my cousin Paul. He had always made me the butt of his jokes and I had learned to ignore him, at least outwardly.

Everything went smoothly at first. We were only doing a small part of the book. No one was in a laughing mood as we all had chores to do after school. My son, 'Jim Lad', suddenly looked at me with a shining, smiley face and said in a posh voice: 'Hello, Mummy!' I turned away, stuffing my fist in my mouth in an effort to stop the uncontrollable snorts of laughter that threatened to explode through my fingers. It was an impossible task.

'Stand up and sit down!' bellowed our teacher. At once everyone did exactly that. Repeatedly. It was pandemonium.

'Order! *Order*!' he shouted over and over but to no avail. No one took any notice and when the bell went we all put our coats on and went home. I had to tell my mother what had happened.

'It's a good job it's the weekend,' she laughed. 'By Monday it'll be a thing of the past. It's a bad choice picking you for a mother, especially an old one. You look like you're still in the baby class!'

I picked up the hat I had been given which was supposed to transform me into Jim Lad's mother and put it on, pulling it down over one eye. I turned to my mother with crossed eyes.

'Aah! Jim Lad! I be yer mother, Mrs Whistler!' I croaked. My poor mother collapsed with laughter, holding her sides and gasping for breath.

'Oh, stop!' she groaned. 'I bet you're the cause of all this trouble! I bet you egged them on, putting on a righteous face! You'd be enough to make a cat laugh!' This made me laugh all over again.

I quite expected the play to be cancelled and hoped it would be. It was very rare that we found anything to amuse us at school. We got through our day wondering what the afternoon would bring. One hour before the bell, we were told to get out *Treasure Island*. We were then handed slips of paper with our names and our parts, also the words we were to speak. There weren't many. This won't be hard, I thought. Looking up, I caught my 'son's' eye. He looked more disreputable than ever. The soles were peeling off his daps, which were soaking wet with the rain, and he had no socks on. He had thin baggy shorts on legs that were skinny and white and he was still wearing his holey jumper, which someone had tried to cobble together. His hair stood up in spikes and yet his eyes were bright and full of fun. So what if he laughs, I thought, it's better than crying. Suddenly I was overwhelmed with realisation. I knew that he had had more than enough tears and this was his way of coping.

As we came to our piece, there was a noise at the door. Someone was coming. I looked up fearfully and in came Jim Lad, grinning.

'Aah, Jim Lad,' I said in as squawky a voice as I could

manage. 'Where have you bin, my son? I bin sittin' yer all night worritin about yer … all night long.' I gave a sob as I said this, which made me cough and once I had started I could not stop. On and on I coughed. My eyes were streaming and so was my nose. Picking up the edge of my ragged sack pinny, I dabbed at my eyes. As I walked towards my son, I tripped on the hem and fell into the cardboard fireplace. Fortunately, the fire was just pretend. My dear son promptly let out the most enormous snort of laughter and we all joined in. I had thought that I was all laughed out but no, there was still plenty there. The play was abandoned and we never put on another. I never saw 'Jim Lad' again after we all left school. Someone who knew him well told me that he moved to London and used to sit outside the Tower of London on the bridge, looking very artistic with his polka dot scarf and his fedora hat, sketching portraits of passers-by. I am told that they were very good. Whether or not this was true I do not know but it does seem like the sort of thing he would do. Anyway, I hope he has had a good life and is still laughing somewhere.

The days spent at school seemed never ending and I longed for the afternoon to come so I could run home to be with my family and feel secure, happy and relaxed in their company. The school holidays were something I really looked forward to. Long joyous days filled with fun and laughter could not come soon enough. Although I saw very few people apart from my family and the travelling Gypsies who visited, I never felt that anything was missing from my life. There was always something going on and the days sped by. Each family on the camp lived their own lives and yet somehow were part of everyone else's. We never needed an excuse for a sing-song or a little dance. As I write, I am reminded of my Aunt Nellie and her kilt.

Nellie was hugely fat but would still get up to dance. We clapped as she whirled and clicked her heels, swirling her kilt above her chubby knees. Round and round she whirled, her thick stockings held up by bits of elastic slipped down into her shoes. Nellie took no notice but with a final whirl of her kilt, she collapsed into her chair, mopping her face. She would look around.

'Where's my Jarge?' she asked and, raising her voice, she called, 'Jarge! Jarge! Where 'e be? I 'opes yer sin that dance cuz I don't think I kin do another!'

'That wuz grand, My Nell!' he called from the back of the small crowd who had gathered round to watch Nellie. 'You looks beautiful my gal!'

Nellie was satisfied and nodded at my mother.

'Not long fer me next kilt, Mary. I'm 'specting yer over 'ome as soon as yer gits the chance to measure me up! I think I might've lost a bit o' weight. I feels a bit thinner an' Jarge says 'e thought 'e could feel me ribs last night. I don't wanna git too skinny. My Jarge likes me a bit chubby.'

Mum tried to keep a straight face but she had a keen sense of the ridiculous. She turned her giggles into a bout of coughing.

'Dear, dear our Mary,' said Nellie, 'You'm too skinny.

I allus said yer needs some fat on yer bones. You mind yer take somethin' fer that cough.'

'Yes, I will Nellie!' said Mum, mopping her streaming eyes. Mum remembered Nellie's last kilt, her once-a-year extravagance. Mum would measure Nellie for her kilt and Nellie would take the measurements to the tailors who would hand-make it for her. This item of clothing was the only thing she wore for the whole year – that and a clean blouse and her 'smalls'. The kilt was always a thing of beauty, a real Scot's kilt. Nellie would save all year to buy it. 'One hundred pounds' she said. Well, it was a lot of money anyway. Mum remembered with tears in her eyes how Nellie had sat in her old chair for Jarge to come in and see her in all her glory and how Jarge, on seeing her, fell to his knees. 'Oh, Nell, yer looks beautiful my gal!'

Nellie dimpled like a young maiden and replied, 'Oh, Jarge!'

Then she had turned to my mother and said, 'See? I told yer Mary. My Jarge likes me to dress up an' look beautiful!'

My mother told me that at that moment she did look beautiful. Jarge certainly thought so.

Some of the most vivid and memorable happenings in our young lives were the wagon burnings. It doesn't happen now, but I saw two. One was my Aunt Prissy's beautiful vardoe. My young cousins' home and inheritance was destroyed while they watched. The effect of this trauma, added to their grief, can only be imagined. There was no time for sentiment. There were four daughters and only one vardoe. The burning ended the possibility of any quarrels.

A few years later I saw another. It was a warm summer night and not quite dark when my parents told me they were both going out for a bit. This was very unusual.

'We won't be long, Rosie,' said Dad.

'Where are you going?'

'Only as far as Aunt Gracie's.'

'Why?'

'Oh, let 'er come along,' said Dad. 'She won't come to no 'arm.'

'But why are we going?' I asked again.

'It's only a big fire,' said Nelson casually.

Fairly satisfied, I asked no more questions, although I did wonder why we had to go down the lane to see a fire when we had a campfire in our own yard. We followed Mum and Dad closely. It was darker now. The sky was full of stars and a sickle moon hung above me. We walked almost in silence, holding my parents' hands looking at the stars. I loved the stars and I tried to count them but there were too many. I saw lots more people walking quietly down the lane and we joined a small crowd of others waiting in a semi-circle by a large vardoe. Suddenly a light was put to a campfire, which blazed up and lit the scene. It was still strangely quiet for such a gathering and there was a sense of anticipation in the air. Then I noticed Granfer for the first time, his leathery features lit up in the firelight.

'Granfer!' I shouted.

Mum squeezed my hand firmly and hushed me quiet. Granfer took no notice of me at any rate, and then he took a blazing branch which a younger man offered him. He stood quietly for a few moments with his head bowed and then threw the burning torch in through the open door of the vardoe. In seconds it was alight. Sparks flew upwards and smoke rose into the sky. There was a unanimous groan from the crowd and then wailing, sobbing and heart-breaking cries were heard all around me. I asked no questions. I remembered what had happened when Aunt Prissy's wagon had been burned. It did not take long for the fire to burn itself out. We all stayed until the last embers glowed on the ground and we walked slowly back home.

Later on in my life, I asked my mother who the vardoe had belonged to. I was told that it was a young single man, a distant relative who had become ill with a wasting disease and had died within six months. The wagon was burned to make sure no infection was passed on, so they said. Wagon burning came to an end, which made sense considering the cost of trailers today.

Although we had little money we did not lack entertainment. We made our own. My Granfer, as far as I know, never went to the pictures until he found himself stranded for some reason in town for a couple of hours. While waiting to be collected he decided to go to the cinema. Being unable to read, he had no idea what the film was or who was in it. When he came home we were all waiting for him. We did not know where he had been and were mostly worried about him as it was getting

quite late. When he sauntered into the yard we surrounded him.

'Granfer! Where've you been?' we all clamoured
around him. 'We were all worried!'

'Aah!' Granfer chuckled, 'I bin to the pictures! It was
all about a woman who was 'alf woman, 'alf fish!'

We were amazed and bombarded him with questions.

'Granfer! How could a woman be half fish?'

'What bit of her was fish?'

Granfer seemed to be enjoying all the attention and
he took off his hat and scratched his head thoughtfully.

'Well now, the top of 'er was a beautiful young
woman,' he said, 'the other bit where 'er legs should be
was a lovely fish tail!'

Granny made Granfer come inside and sit down and
we all followed.

'Yer my Edwin, 'ave a cuppa tea an' a bit o' toasted
bread and butter and sit yerself by the fire. I wants to yer
all about this fishy woman meself!'

Granfer laughed.

''Ee be worse than these young chavvies, Mary Ann!'

Granny had never been to the pictures and could not
wait to hear the story. We all gathered round on the
rugs, hardly daring to breathe. When he had taken a sip
and a mouthful or two he began.

'Hurry up Granfer!' someone shouted, 'we can't wait
no more!'

We were almost jumping up and down. Granfer took
out his hanky. We knew he was teasing us so we sat as
still as mice.

''Ee'll 'ave to wait a bit longer,' he said, patting each

of his pockets, one by one. 'I can't start 'til I've 'ad me pinch o' snuff. I can't find it Mary Ann. I reckon I lost it in the pictures. I ain't 'ad me snuff yet. I dunno where me snuff box is ...'

'Oh, stop, my Edwin!' said Granny, almost stamping her foot, 'and tell us all about the fish woman!'

'Oh all right,' sighed Granfer. 'Well, I don't know 'ow she come to be 'alf fish and 'alf woman but she was real pretty. With a nice set o' teeth an' a nice laugh. I think the young man went fishin' with 'is nets an' catched 'er.'

Granfer scratched his nose. 'Or did she save un from drownin'?'

'*Granfer!*'

'Well, anyhow, 'e thought she was right pretty and took 'er 'ome with 'im an' they 'ad all sorts o' good times.'

'What sort o' good times?' asked Granny suspiciously.

''E took 'er to a dance!'

''Ow could she dance wi' no legs?' Granny scoffed.

'Well, she 'ad a long frock on an' 'e sort o' carried 'er about an' pushed 'er in a wheelchair.'

'Didn't that look funny?' said Granny.

'She was so beautiful once 'er 'air 'ad dried out a bit. It was nearly touchin' 'er toes – or at least where 'er toes would o' bin if she 'ad 'em.'

Our mouths dropped open at this. Granfer continued.

''Er eyes were big an' as beautiful as could be. And 'er lashes were that long, they made shadders on 'er cheeks.'

We all gazed at Granfer, almost intoxicated by the vision of beauty he had described to us.

'Ooh, I wish I 'ad bin there!' we all said.

'So do I!' said Granny. Granfer paused and sipped his tea.

'After a bit, she wanted legs but there was no way to give 'er 'em. So after all sorts o' goin's on, the young man decides praps it'd be best if 'e put 'er back in the sea. So one sunny day, 'e puts 'er in 'is boat and took 'er back to the big rock where 'e found 'er an' they says goodbye to each other. There was a lot o' singin' an' all sorts o' music. I never 'eard the like,' Granfer whispered, 'it was all sort o' magical. The fish woman, they called 'er a mermaid, 'ad big tears rollin' down 'er cheeks an' so did the young man.'

'What happened Granfer?'

'All of a sudden, a very 'andsome young man swam up to the rock and some 'ow clambers up with 'is fish tail an' 'olds 'is arms out to 'er. She slips into the water an' swam towards 'im. Then they kissed each other an' there was a lot more music an' singin' and then – they was all gone.'

Granfer sat back in his armchair and sighed happily.

'Aah. It were lovely.'

'Yes it were very lovely!' we all said.

''Ow did they ever find they fish people?' asked Granny.

Well, that set a problem. We had never heard of this before.

'Did you think they was real then?' asked Aunt Mary, 'I don't think there are real fish people, Dad, it's only false.'

'Well if it was false, I couldn't see where it was joined

54

on,' said Granfer, 'I 'ad on me glasses but they were no 'elp!'

We glanced at each other and giggled.

'No,' said Aunt Mary, dryly, 'I don't 'spect they would be.'

'I do 'member the mermaid's name though,' said Granfer.

'Ooh, what was it? Tell me!' urged Granny.

'It were "Miranda". She were a beautiful young woman but I couldn't be doin' with the tail. I do like a bit o' salmon but I don't like a woman with a fishy smell, even if she is beautiful!'

''Ow do we know she smelt fishy, my Edwin?'

'Well I don't think anybuddy mentioned it. I noticed some o' the young gals looked a bit jealous of 'er 'cause she were more beautiful than they was. They'd take out their hankies an' put 'em up to their noses an' if she got a bit near, they'd move away, twitchin' their faces.'

'Well,' said Granny in a matter-of-fact voice, 'she was better off with 'er own kind is what I always says. It's best to stay with the folks 'ee knows.'

Granny never wanted any of her children to marry 'out' to a gadje because she felt it was better to keep families together. We all knew our own ways and it was much easier for everyone. Even Miranda understood that. We were too young to realise that Granny may have been wrong about this, or that when we were older we would have a choice. I have never seen the film *Miranda*, although it has been on TV many times. Granfer made it seem so magical that nothing else I saw could come close to it.

Granfer had suffered with bronchitis for many years. It was worse in the winter. When spring came, Granfer became his old self. The day he died came as a shock to all of us. That morning, my Aunt Mary was trying to do six jobs at once as usual.

'Yer, Rosie. Take yer Granfer 'is cuppa tea.'

'Yes,' I said. 'Of course.'

Granfer was lying back on his pillows, eyes closed.

'Cup of tea, Granfer.'

'Oh, thank 'ee my pretty,' he said gently. Aunt Mary came in behind me so I moved to let her through.

'Yer, Dad. I've toasted you a lovely bit o' bread with fresh butter,' she said. I heard her give a sudden gasp.

'Dad? Dad?' she said. Then gently pushing me out of the room I heard her say, 'Mam! Oh Mam, Dad's gone!'

For a moment there was utter silence. Granny went in to see Granfer. I heard her whisper.

'Edwin, oh my Edwin!'

Granfer would never call her 'my Mary Ann' again. He had left us as gently and calmly as he had lived. He had left a huge gap in our lives and I have never stopped missing him. Whenever we talk of him, one or other of us will say, 'I really loved that old man.' We all smile and say, 'We all loved him.'

Granfer's death had come as a huge shock and it seemed that time should stand still. And yet life and work had to go on as before. The only real change was that the camp now had 'the 'lectrics' as Granny called it. When Granny finally got 'the 'lectric' our joy was unconfined. We all had at least one electric light and power socket. Granny had two lights in her hut, which nearly drove her mad. The little ones could not resist the 'magic' of the ''lectric light'. On off, on off.

'Stop! Go and play!' Dad shouted. It was more than a week before the novelty wore off.

When Uncle Alfie brought back a telly, everyone was amazed that the picture was in black and white. The aerial was dodgy. It frequently 'snowed' even when the sun was out. Aunt Britt went out to fetch in her washing when it was 'pouring' on telly, only to find that it was a brilliantly sunny day outside. This happened a few times until she got used to it.

'Mary,' she confided to Mum one day, 'I felt such a fool!'

Mum laughed but she never let on that she had been fooled as well. When the Coronation was aired we all crowded round to watch, squashing on Granny's sofa or hugging our knees on the rugs. Some even got dressed up for the occasion as though they were actually attending in person. We listened to the commentary almost in silence except for the odd remark.

'Well,' said one, 'she's a lot prettier than I thought.'

'Ooh! Look at all they church men – all that gold an' they still wants a c'lection from all they poor folk!'

'Look at the jewels!'

'Fancy sittin' down fer yer grub with all that stuff on yer 'ead! It's enough to make yer 'ead ache!'

Everyone had something to say. It seemed to last for ever, yet we were still sorry when it was over.

'Well,' we said, 'fancy bein' on telly. Granfer would never 'ave believed it!'

The tiny ones thought that the people were somehow in the box and tried peering around the back of the set. It reminded me of when I was little and thought that people lived in the wireless. I tried to explain it to them but it was not easy to do when I did not fully understand myself. We ended the day by chatting, telling jokes and having a little party. Everyone brought something and all had a good time. I could not help but smile as I thought of Granfer marvelling over the wonder of the cinema screen. How amazed he would have been to think he could have sat in his own armchair and watched the Queen in his own home!

4

Wild Rosemary

I lived on Granny's 'bit o' ground' until I married my husband John when I was eighteen years old. I had ventured out from the Romany encampment where I grew up when I was just sixteen and travelled each day by bus into Weston-Super-Mare to work in Woolworths. It was my first real connection with the world outside school and my family life in the camp. My life now had a new aspect to it: another 'compartment'.

My life working on the sweet counter was a whole new experience for me. I learned quickly and soon settled into my daily routine and got used to the different faces around me at work. I first met John when he came into the shop for a cup of tea. I had seen him once or twice before at our camp on a pushbike – poking around my father's scrap yard for bits and pieces, I expect. He was very slim with brown eyes and had dark hair slicked back with Brylcreem like all the young lads back then. He always looked smart, I thought, though I had no interest in any young man at the time – I had more than enough interests as it was! He would linger over the pick 'n' mix while casting meaningful glances in my direction.

'Come to the pictures?' he would ask me, over and over. '*Prize of Gold* is on with Mai Zetterling and Richard Widmark.'

'Where?'

'The Odeon or the Central. Go on. Come with me.'

'I don't know you,' I tried.

'Well, how are you going to get to know me if you don't walk out with me?'

There seemed to be a certain logic in this.

The first time I took John home, Granny looked fiercely at him and said, 'Go 'ome young man! Our Rosie's much too nice fer 'ee! Go 'ome!' John, not realising that Granny never joked about serious matters, just laughed. He got on very well with my family, though, so in the end she accepted him, especially as John often brought little treats that he shared with Granny as well.

My family grew very fond of John; my father especially so, as he could see how clever he was with his hands and how he was always willing to help in any way. The boys also liked him because he joined in with any project that they were engaged in and took them on trips to London when he drove on long-distance trips in his lorry. He won my mother over when he took his coat off and dug her garden over for her and helped her with other little jobs.

Before I knew it, I was engaged to be married. It was quite common in the fifties to get married at sixteen or seventeen. So I was married in 1956. Most of John's

60

family had emigrated to Australia as 'ten-pound Pommies' after the war but he had not wanted to leave England. When we read the rules regarding the dos and don'ts of getting married, I was a bit surprised that as I did not live within the parish where we were to marry, I did not qualify. John lived with his Gran in the town so that was all right.

'It'll be fine,' said John, 'you can stay with my Aunt Flo for the few weeks to qualify.'

'Oh, all right,' I agreed unwillingly. Aunt Flo was kind and sometimes funny but her house, although painfully clean, was dark and so quiet! I was not used to this. I was used to all sorts of happy sounds of singing, laughter and chatter. I was glad to go to work in the mornings where the girls were bright and chatty, singing away with each other as happy as could be. Aunt Flo lived near the town centre so it wasn't far to walk. I rarely had more than a slice of toast and a cup of tea for breakfast, although Aunt Flo served fried bread and baked beans. I was forced to get John to speak to her.

'Tell her I don't eat breakfast and *never* fried bread. I won't fit into my wedding dress if I eat that every morning!'

John told Aunt Flo that I had never tasted baked beans or eaten fried bread. She was surprised and, when she asked me, I told her that we always ate our own homegrown vegetables at home and our own chickens and eggs. Aunt Flo was not a very good cook.

'Eat up Rosie,' she said at Sunday lunch. I tried but I was thinking about my parents and my brothers eating my mother's delicious roast potatoes, slowly cooked around the joint with the freshest vegetables, fit for a king, from Dad's garden. My mother's gravy was the best I have tasted, full of rich flavour. Aunt Flo's was made from flour and water. It was edible but I envied my family's lovely dinner.

'I enjoyed that Aunty Flo,' I said untruthfully, but I could not add anything else.

Aunty Flo was a quiet, almost depressing person. She was not even John's real aunt. I could chat to anyone but I found her very hard going. I only had to stay with her for a few weeks, but it was a very long few weeks. I was almost eighteen and very innocent. Aunt Flo seemed to sense this and, probably feeling that someone should tell me about the facts of life, proceeded to sit me down and inform me of the intimacy (or lack of it) in her own marriage. It turned out to be no marriage at all and I sat in absolute embarrassment, not knowing what to say. As young as I was, I knew there was more to a marriage than this sham. She seemed to think that she had told me all that I needed to know and went to make a cup of tea. The last couple of weeks were an embarrassing nightmare. I tried to avoid her eyes at all cost and I could not bring myself to even *speak* to Uncle Bill if he entered the room. She, in her way, thought that she had done me a favour in letting me in on the secrets of procreation. She kept giving me little smiles of encouragement and pats on the shoulder. How could she know that after seeing our animals begetting and giving birth to their offspring that I was not completely in the dark? If anything, I was far better informed than she was. I was not a bit surprised that she had never had a child.

It would have been an impossibility or a miracle. How sad, I thought.

I visited my family several times a week during the time I spent at Aunty Flo's. I cannot say that I enjoyed those weeks but I made the best of them and slowly got through the days.

The day before my wedding, I broke the zip on the pretty dress I had bought to change into for after the reception. This was a disaster. I was in tears. I had tried it on and it had split apart as I was taking it off. Later on that day, John's friend Reg popped in with a message for John. He asked how things were going with our plans and I told him what had happened to my dress.

'Give it here, I'll fix it,' he said. I did not think he could but he did, just in time.

My father gave me away. 'Don't she look lovely?' he said to everyone who would listen as I stood in my pretty white dress and silver shoes.

'Yes,' said Mum. 'She looks beautiful.'

It had cost eight pounds for the dress and veil. My whole week's wages was only seven pounds. My friend Denise who worked with me in Woolworths was my Maid of Honour and my Aunt Rene and Uncle Nelson's beautiful daughter Brenda was my bridesmaid. Her little face glowed when I asked her.

'Thanks, Rosie! Yes, I will!' she said and so she was.

Granny in Town, my maternal grandmother who was a gadje, gave me a modest reception in her own home and made me a beautiful two-tier cake.

'Oh, thank you Granny! You've made me a wonderful cake. Do you remember when I was about five or six and I expected you to give me a slice of the wedding cake you had made for a friend's wedding?' I asked her.

'Yes,' she laughed, 'I do. You never stopped talking about it to your mother. You couldn't understand why you couldn't have just one slice!'

I remembered all the cakes and tarts Granny in Town had made for us over the years and what a kind and understanding woman she was. Whatever her true feelings about my mother marrying a Gypsy and living on a Gypsy encampment, she never allowed anything at all to come between us and showed her love on many occasions. We loved her in return. I often think of that dear little person.

My father, who was as a rule very quiet when he met Granny in Town, admired the cake.

'Rosemary looks as pretty as a spring day!' she said to him. When he realised she meant 'Rosie' he beamed all over his face and repeated it to all who would listen.

To my knowledge Gypsy Granny never went to any weddings, although she went to all the funerals. Perhaps she felt if she didn't go, the marriage wouldn't take place. She hadn't wanted any of her children to get married because she wanted them to stay as her children alone, but once they were married she completely accepted the situation. So I did not expect her to come to my wedding; she did give me a beautiful antique vase as a wedding present though, so that was a sign of her acceptance.

When I am asked what I think about the television show *My Big Fat Gypsy Wedding*, I hardly know what to say. It is all completely alien to me. I can just see my father's face if I had put on a dress so huge that walking was an impossibility, sitting down even worse and as for going to the toilet – well, it doesn't bear thinking about! I have always felt that a wedding dress should be comfortable as well as beautiful. My father hated wearing new clothes, especially new shirts or shoes.

'Give us me old pair o' shoes, Mary,' he used to say to my mother, 'a bit o' polish and they'll do me.' Or he would say, 'That old shirt's got real soft. I don't want they new stiff ones!'

Mum would usually reply, 'Well, I'll have to wash them five or six times before you wear them then.'

'Aye, that's right,' he'd reply.

If Dad went to a wedding he refused to wear stiff new clothes. No, his best old ones would do. As long as they were fresh and clean, that was all that mattered. Besides, Dad loved what he called 'a bit of a dance'. Not the waltzing or anything modern, but he and my Granfer loved tap dancing or an Irish jig. They would perform these on any occasion, hooting, snapping their fingers and having a whale of a time. When they were exhausted, they would sit down and tell jokes and shaggy dog stories. There would have been no room for massive dresses. The money that they cost would have been way beyond our pockets, and for a dress that would only be worn for one day it would not have even entered our heads.

We could not afford a honeymoon but we had a week off work anyway. John's friend had borrowed his father's huge American car which did about five miles to the gallon. Of course, it ran out of petrol and had to be pushed to a garage. I have never driven a car in my life but I had to steer while they pushed. It is a good job that there was very little traffic on the roads then or we would never have reached our destination!

Since we weren't able to have everyone to the reception on our wedding day because there was not enough room, we made up for it afterwards. We had a big get-together at Granny's place and laughed, chatted, got a little tipsy and recalled memories of our childhood.

At the party, I spotted Granny's fox fur stole hanging over the partition wall in its usual place. Violet pulled it down and threw it around her shoulders. Assuming a haughty air she strolled around the room looking down her nose.

'Ugh! Take it away!' I yelled. I hated the thing. It had frightened me for years.

'Why? It's dead,' said Violet. I always thought it was looking at me. Wherever I moved, its beady eyes followed. I used to have terrible nightmares about it when I was a child. One night I dreamed the fox was talking to me.

'How would *you* like to be hung over a wall?' he demanded, 'and how would you like it if a bad child tried to pull *your* eyes out?'

I must admit this is something I had tried to do. I could not bear his glassy eyes and had made several attempts to remove them. I awoke during this dream to find I had got out of bed and was running barefoot around the yard. My father came out and caught me.

'Don't tell me yer be startin' runnin' round at night,

Rosie! It be bad enough when Rosina gets up to her tricks!'

My cousin Rosina often had bad dreams, which resulted in her standing on top of the chicken house in the middle of the night, crying out at the top of her voice.

'Ohh,' I sobbed, 'Granny's fox caught me and hung me over the wall 'cause he wanted his eyes back!'

'It's only a bad dream,' Mum said, coaxing me back to bed, 'but leave the fox's eyes alone in future.'

I did, but I never quite got over my fear of Mr Fox. Everyone at the party laughed when they heard about it.

'Fancy being afraid of an old dead fox,' they said.

'Well I'm not now, but when you are little, anything seems possible.'

Yes, we found great pleasure in our own company. We had our little ups and downs but we never held grudges. We were all too chatty for that.

5

Baby's Breath

John and I had a small rented flat for the first few months of our marriage but were forced to leave it, as it was full of mice. We had to clap our hands at the kitchen door to frighten the mice away. Our next home was a brand new purpose-built council flat. We had very little money but John insisted on buying me a new twin-tub washing machine. I was a little reticent at first, when I remembered the washing machine my father had brought home for my mother. She told him that it was harder work than scrubbing by hand. The twin-tub was hard work too. I had to hold the rinsing hose over the sink when it was ready to drain or it would rear up and shower the kitchen and me. When it spun, I had to brace my whole body against it to prevent it walking across the room and if I forgot to place the little rubber mat on top of the spinner, the lid would pop up and fling the washing around the kitchen. The old lady from the flat below came up to see what was going on one washday and caught me fighting with the machine.

'What larks!' she shrieked, throwing herself on the sofa, sending me into a collapse of laughter, 'What larks!'

We had a small balcony where I could hang the washing and a Radiant oil stove for heating if we ran out of coal. The oil was in a little bottle, which we had to put in upside down. The nozzle needed a little extra pressure so we fixed this with the aid of two old pennies. It worked very well. We never had much money in those days and pay was very poor. We were always broke by payday. One day I did not have enough money to buy a loaf of bread. Well, I thought, I'll use the pennies in the oil heater! I took them out and gave them a good wash. They still smelled a bit but I bought my bread and nothing was said. John laughed until he cried when I told him. We never used the heater again and I have never been that hard up since.

Being married and living in a flat was, surprisingly, not very different from living in a wagon. There were a lot of steps to climb and I had to walk up a steep hill to get to it after work, which I soon got used to. The rooms were larger, of course, with very high ceilings and it seemed harder to keep tidy because of this. There was more room to leave things lying around and not always put them in their proper place. We soon realised that we would be in a big muddle so we began to live by the adage 'Don't put it down, put it away.' It surprised me that the same rules applied in a flat as they did in a caravan. Also, bigger rooms are much harder to keep warm, not like our cosy little wagon with its glowing hot range. We had an open grate in the new flat, which heated the water as well as the rooms when we had a fire going. We needed a lot more furniture to fill the two-bedroom flat, which was more expense, but the family helped out. The rent was less than two pounds a week but with food and other expenses it was difficult to make ends meet. John decided that I was a better money manager than he was after a while, then things became a great deal easier. I missed the warmth of our wagon and sitting in front of it with hot toast and mugs of tea. The memory of the singing, chatting and laughter that came from Granny's place brought such a feeling of comfort that I have never known since. I never felt fully at home in the gadje world, but as I still saw a good deal of my Romany family, I never let it bother me. I could always go and visit 'up home' if I wanted to and if my cousins were home we behaved as though we were still children, laughing and chattering.

Granny lived on for several years after Granfer died. She was never the same and gradually let her gals, as she called them, take over. Aunt Betsy, Aunt Amy, Britt and Mary took care of Granny and Uncle Alfie quite beautifully. Granny still cracked the whip though.

'Come on you gals, the mats want a good scrub! Is the taters peeled fer our supper yet?'

She was getting slower and slower though and one day she was struck down with a severe stroke, which rendered her unconscious. She never awoke from it. She stayed at home in her own bed, looked after by her family. When I went to see her, she looked at peace and sleeping. I watched her for a long time, remembering how strong and active she had always been; the hours we had spent collecting herbs, fruit and mushrooms for her, and now she was dying.

Her funeral was huge. Travellers from all over the country came and brought flowers and wreaths. The church was full to overflowing and the bare earth covering Granny's grave was heaped with flowers as it had been at Granfer's funeral. I felt sad but I was glad she was buried with her Edwin. The funeral went on for hours. There was laughter and tears while Granny and Granfer were remembered with love.

Romany funerals were always very extravagant because Romany families came from all over the country to be there. Each one brought a wreath with the name of the deceased or a picture of their wagon; perhaps something they used to make or sell. If the deceased man or woman had been from a well-known family and equally well-respected he or she would often be called a 'Gypsy King' or a 'Gypsy Queen'. The horse-drawn vardoes would stop over until the next day. All would catch up on the news; who was married or had children since the last meeting. There were tears of course, but also smiles and jokes. Everyone knew that life must go on and it did not mean that anyone loved was forgotten. On the contrary, even dozens of years after our loved ones have died, they are still brought to mind at family gatherings. Maybe someone will sing a song or tell a joke and someone else will say, 'Hey, don't that 'mind yer of Granny?' Another will perform a jig and a voice will pipe up, 'Oh my, who do that 'mind yer of?' So funerals can be happy occasions as well as sad. The next day, everybody helped to clear away the rubbish that had been left behind and shared a meal and a cup of tea, then off the wagons would go, horses tied to the back and the lurcher dogs running alongside. The older men led the horses at the head while the pans and kettles clattered away at the back in the kettle box. It would take a long time for this caravan of wagons to vanish from sight, a sight that cannot be seen today.

A very strange thing happened in the few days after Granny died. Everyone had gone to the wake except Mum, who was feeling poorly and had stayed at home. She thought she would light the range and make a piece of toast. Opening her door, she stepped outside. Suddenly she saw the light in Granny's hut flick on and off. This was repeated again and again and then stopped. Mum was not scared. She thought perhaps one of the young ones was up to mischief. She walked across the yard and slid open the heavy wooden door to Granny's place, expecting to see one of the family come home early. All was quiet and dark. My mother was tiny but did not have one nervous bone in her body. She called out.

'Hello? Anyone there?'

There was no reply. Puzzled, she collected her coal and lit her fire. She watched the door of Granny's place until everyone came home.

'It's a pity you felt bad, Mary. You was the only one missing,' said Dad when he came in.

'The only one?' Mum asked.

'Yes. I stood by the door and counted everyone in. It was a good turnout.'

For the first time, Mum felt afraid. Should she tell

or not? Well, she thought, nothing's harmed me so say nothing. I was the only one she told, many years later. Logic tells me that there was a fault in the electricity supply but it never happened again.

After she died and until his own death, Uncle Alfie lived alone in Granny's place, as we called it, a large wooden hut converted from a chicken house which she had made warm and comfortable. All the family had congregated there on many occasions and it was still the hub of family get-togethers for a long time after. It was open to all and Granny had dished up many a meal to a passing relative. I still remember Granfer and my father doing an Irish jig there, everyone clapping and encouraging them. Small children should not have been there but if we kept quiet we remained unnoticed and enjoyed every minute.

Very little had changed in the camp: if you had walked into it at any time of the day in any decade from the thirties to the seventies, you would think you had travelled back in time. As soon as I came in through the gate, I was home. It was quite a different feeling walking in through my own front door. It was only after Sarah was born that I really settled down. We were then a proper family.

Sarah was my first child, born three years after my marriage. Then three years later we had a little son. We called him Shane. He lived just one day. He had been born with a congenital heart defect. That was a terrible time for all of us. A year later our beautiful daughter

Virginia was born. She had flaxen hair and sparkling blue eyes. She took after John's sister Mary in colouring. Sarah adored her new baby sister and they became very close. Virginia grew into a lovely woman, kind and generous and very loving. She died aged forty-eight in tragic circumstances in the Dominican Republic over a year ago. We miss her so much. Finally, when Virginia was eight years old, we had our baby twins, Daniel and Claire. They were such a joy to us and filled all our lives with pleasure.

When Virginia was born we moved into a newly built house not far from the flat. It was January 1964 when we moved in. There was no heating in one of the worst winters that I could remember since the one in 1947. The pipes had frozen and Sarah was put to bed in her dressing gown, Virginia in a sleeping bag. We managed to get a fire going but it was freezing. There was no central heating back then, or double-glazing, but we made the best of it as I had been taught. After the twins were born we moved into a four-bedroom house just round the corner. That *did* have central heating.

I loved having my children. Every day was fun. In the summer I took them somewhere each day; the beach, the swimming pool, on picnics, nothing that cost any money. I would show them the squirrels in the park and the fish in the pond. John told them the names of all the birds and often brought home a half-dead rabbit, crow or owl that he had come across on the road while he was lorry driving. He would show the children how to nurse them back to health until they could be set free. At times we would have wood mice and hedgehogs in the garden. We would sit quietly in the warm summer dusk and watch the mother and baby hedgehogs tumble about in the grass. I would teach them the names of wild flowers and show them not to touch the poisonous ones. In the autumn we would throw ash keys into the air and watch them spin like helicopters. They all grew up with a love of nature and marvelled at the way their surroundings were made and grew in their seasons.

Virginia was a very tactile child. She loved textures and would stroke all sorts of materials – silk, velvet and fur. I remember her being attached to a length of pink satin ribbon that I had bought to tie back her long blonde hair. She became very upset when she realised what it was for.

'No,' she cried, 'If it's in my hair, I won't be able to reach it!'

So I gave in and every night she would lie in bed stroking her piece of satin ribbon until she fell asleep. One hot day, the roses and nasturtiums were full of bees and Virginia was playing in the garden. She was about three at the time. I heard her scream at the top of her voice and I nearly fell over my feet in my rush to reach her.

'Whatever is the matter?' I asked her, holding her in my shaking arms. She just pointed to the ground. Lying dead was a huge bumblebee and Virginia was nursing a badly stung hand.

'Oh Mummy,' she sobbed, 'I didn't mean to die him. He was so soft and furry. I only wanted to stroke his little back!'

'Oh dear. Never mind,' I said, giving her a cuddle.

'I expect everyone feels like that but we mustn't do it or we will hurt them and ourselves. There's lots of little creatures we can cuddle but leave these alone, ok?'

I shall never forget that lovely day and my beautiful daughter finding out the hard way that it is not always a good thing to love unwisely.

Yes, I was brought up with the love of the country-side and the animals, birds, insects; everything was given to us freely by God and we were told that we must respect them and their feelings. If they hurt us, it was only because they were trying to protect themselves.

Little things stand out in my mind, mainly because they only happened once and yet were so amazing. We had had a hard winter. It froze hard overnight for days on end. The children said there was frost on their windows in the morning.

'You will know what cold really is when it freezes *inside* your window!' I said. That is what happened to us one year in our vardoe. Dad kept the fire going day and night but that winter of 1947–1948 was one of the coldest that many people had ever experienced. Many died of cold and lack of good food that winter. I remember my mother reading the paper aloud to my father.

'Oh dear,' I heard her say, 'people in Germany are dying of cold in their beds!'

'Well they must blame 'Itler fer their troubles!' said Dad. I shuddered with horror. I could imagine only too well how it must have felt to freeze to death. I awoke quite early one freezing day. I could hear the steady dripping of water. I did not realise it but we were having a thaw. That had happened a few times and then it froze again even harder. I went outside. The sun was up and it seemed a bit warmer. Suddenly, I heard a tinkling sound and I saw a very beautiful sight. The ice on a big tree had thawed just enough so that the icicles fell from the branches all at once. As they fell, the sun shone through it and it looked and sparkled like crystal – blues, greens and yellows. Perhaps it only lasted for seconds but the beauty of it was forever stamped on my memory. I have tried to describe the wonder of it many times but have never been able to do it justice. Every winter that passes renews and refreshes that wondrous vision of a rainbow falling to earth.

My Granny and Granfer had died by the time Sarah was born but they still seemed to be part of our lives. The feeling was very strong. When my children saw the photograph of Granfer with some of his grandchildren they gasped, 'Oh Mum, what a lot of children.' There sat Granfer, on the wagon steps, surrounded by children. Granny had often ruefully commented to my mother, 'Well Mary, you'm never short o' company. Sometimes I feels like 'idin' away but I ain't got the room!' Many a posy of wild flowers was pressed into her hard-working hands by a scruffy little child. She was just pleased that they had thought of their Granny. She would not have wanted to be alone, and until the day they both died they were encircled with the love of the family.

On the camp we would visit each family home in turn. Uncle Alfie spoke in a gruff voice and when Virginia was a baby she was frightened by it, but she quickly got over that and told him how much she loved him, which pleased him no end. Uncle Fred, young Betsy's dad, was a quiet man but when we were young he always had time for us children. He let us hold the newborn pig-lets 'just fer a minute or the Mammy pig will get upset,' he said. It was he who allowed our four-year-old Virginia to twist him around her little finger as he stood patiently holding the ladder so that she could pick blackberries.

'How is Uncle Fred?' was almost the first thing she said when we took her there. At the first opportunity she would race off to see him, sure as she always was of a welcome. She loved him very much. Even much later, after she had married and moved away, she always talked about her Uncle Fred and asked how he was.

Sarah loved everyone, but her Granny came before everyone else, even her Granfer who doted on her and gave her bits off his plate while he sang old songs.

'Granfer, sing "pickin' a chicken with me" please, Granfer!' she would beg. She would make him sing it over and over again until he said, 'I've got no voice left now!'

Looking back, I think some of the changes the modern world has brought are not always for the better. Some things are irreplaceable and their value not always real-ised at the time. My father had mentioned several times that he was planning on buying a much larger vardoe. More modern, he said, with a living area, bedroom and a nice kitchenette. Just the right size for himself and my mother. We children were all married by then. Sarah was almost four and Virginia about eighteen months old. My parents' new home was not going to be brand new, Dad said, but nice and comfortable. Mum would still have a little range in the living area, 'To toast yer bread on, Mary,' he said. Mum did not say very much. She usually went along with whatever Dad decided; remember, this was around fifty years ago. When I thought about it, it never entered my mind that in order to bring home a much larger vardoe or modern caravan, the old one would have to be disposed of in some way to make room. So when John took me and the girls to the camp at the weekend, I could not believe my eyes. To say I was shocked was an understatement. I just stood, rooted to the spot with a huge lump in my throat. I have never felt so strange in my life.

'What's going on?' I said. 'Why are you breaking up our wagon?'

Several pairs of eyes regarded me in astonishment. Bang, bang. Someone was removing the glass panels that hid the beds; the little wooden bed where my mother had tucked me up, wellies and all after I had well and truly won the wellington war, the pretty corner cupboard where my father kept his shaving mug and brush, even the little mirror over the range had all been taken away or openly exposed.

'But why?' I asked, bewildered. 'Why?'

'There ain't no room fer two wagons,' said Dad. 'It's got to go.'

I remembered my dear mother and the hours she spent on hot summer days up a ladder, painting away and singing to herself. I felt choked. I could hardly speak. Our wagon may not have been an object of beauty to many, and it was very small, but I couldn't help thinking of the winter evenings we had spent in front of a roaring fire, eating bowls of rabbit stew in the light of three candles which threw misty shadows up the walls. I could see Mum sitting in her chair, her face in her hands, weeping because she had no money to feed us and her tearful smile when my little brother Teddy, the only one of us who ever saved any money, tipped his moneybox into her lap.

'I'll pay you back Teddy,' she had said. He, copying the men when they made a sale, replied by shrugging his shoulders, 'That's all right my dear. Any time will do!'

These memories and many more crowded my mind as I watched the demolition of what had been my childhood home. Thinking of this today, I can only say that many a mansion could not hold more memories than that old Gypsy wagon. It would probably be worth thousands of pounds today. My father told me that it had fetched a lot of money sold piecemeal. Even the axles sold for a great deal. I wondered what was more tragic; our little home plundered for its bits and pieces or my Aunt Prissy's truly beautiful wagon burned to the ground for the sake of tradition.

Of course, the modern caravan was much more comfortable and spacious than our old wagon. The living area was quite large with comfy furniture and there was a small but pretty range to one side where my mother could sit on a winter's evening and toast her bread. Having 'the 'lectrics' pleased my mother no end. We still visited as often as before but it was a long time before I stopped looking for our old wagon. I still remember it as though it was yesterday and I am glad that my mother took at least one photograph of me standing on the steps when I was just a baby. I never saw again the crystal door handle that I had played with so often as a child, watching the rainbow colours where it had been struck by the sun. I realise now that I am older and wiser that it probably fetched a good price. I cannot blame my father for getting the best price he could, but it hurt.

'Surely he might have remembered how much I loved that old doorknob and saved it for me?'

'I remembered,' said Mum, 'but one minute it was here and then it was gone. By the time I remembered it again, it was too late. Men don't think the way we do. Your father always kept nice bits and pieces for you that he thought might bring you a bit of money in the future. I'm afraid the little doorknob slipped away unnoticed.'

That was true. My father gave me lots of little things that turned up in boxes of scrap: a little silver pig pin cushion, a broken bracelet and fruit knives. I was glad to be able to sell them to a local antique dealer and they paid for the children's school uniforms throughout their schooldays so I should not mind too much. I know that, had I told my father that I had really wanted it, he would have paid to get it back, but, knowing they needed the money for the new caravan, I said nothing.

'Never mind,' I said, but the loss of the little door-knob is with me still. It was the one object that enabled me to be in the safest place I could be. Warm and comfortable in the loving arms of my family.

When they could afford a television set, they would watch all the sitcoms and make remarks about the way gadje folks lived.

'Ah, that's a pretty gal,' Dad would say.

'And what a handsome young man!' my mother would add.

Most of all though, Dad loved to watch the boxing and he would get quite carried away.

'Ah, Mary. It do remind me of when I'd box at the fairs!'

'Yes,' said my mother, looking at him sideways, 'you didn't always win, Eddy. I spent plenty of time putting plasters on your cuts and bruises!'

Even though Dad loved the novelty of the telly, he would never miss an episode of *The Archers*, never failing to ridicule their farming methods or the 'love bits'.

'What rubbish!' he would say, and 'What a waste o' time!' Yet at seven the next evening he would be counting the seconds until the familiar music told everyone that *The Archers* had started. Not a sound could be heard for the next quarter of an hour. The second it was over, he got up and rammed his trilby on the back of his head and turned off the radio.

'What rubbish! A waste o' time!' and out he would go to the pub.

To think that I used to read Enid Blyton stories to everyone and how they enjoyed them. We never thought that one day the world would come into our little Gypsy homes and we would sit and watch the gadjes' way of life.

My father died when my twins were seven weeks old, but they have always known him. We have made sure of that. I knew that he had just a short time to live. He was fading away before our eyes but I don't think that he knew. If he did, he ignored it. He was eating less and less.

'Give they bits to the ferrets, Mary,' he said to my mother, handing her his almost untouched plate. Mum did not argue. She knew he would not eat another crumb. He still enjoyed his glass of beer though. Mum saw no reason to deprive him of the only thing he still enjoyed. He always looked up at me expectantly when I came to visit him and his eyes lit up when I handed him a box of homemade sausage rolls. He always ate one at once.

'Well, our Rosie,' he would say, 'I don't know 'ow you learned to cook like this, but I'm glad you can!'

Mum told me that he always ate the lot. Our twins were just a few weeks old and Dad adored them.

'Ain't they pretty little things?' he would say, rocking them gently and singing 'Mairzy doats and dozy doats' to them. Children loved my father and he loved them in return.

He was gradually getting worse. Mum had struggled to keep him at home but the doctor insisted he must go to hospital. I went to see him the night before he went in.

'Look in me coat pocket,' he whispered, 'something fer the chavvies.'

In his pocket was a five-pound note (which forty-two years ago was a lot of money).

'Thank you, Dad.'

He winked at me in the old way.

'See you tomorrow Dad.'

'Don't you fergit, mind.'

'As if I would.' I smiled at him but I was choked.

On my way out I returned the money to Mum, thinking she might need it.

Mum went to the hospital every day, as did all of Dad's sisters and brothers. What shocked me most of all was that on his first night in hospital, Dad fell out of bed and cut his head and eyebrow open. He looked dreadful. I thought how safe and cared for he had been at home with my mother and yet the first night away from his home in the care of professionals he had fallen out of bed and hurt himself badly. The nurse in charge was very apologetic. I know accidents happen but I was saddened and disappointed that it had happened this way. My father was not the same afterwards. I used to stand by his bed and hold his hand. Sometimes he smiled but mostly he slept.

The night before he died he seemed a little better.

'Will you get me a glass o' beer Rosie?' he asked me. I knew that he would not be allowed to have it. They were very strict in those days. So I lied.

'Yes, Dad. I'll get you a beer.'

'He'll go to sleep and forget,' said Mum. He died that

night. I have never forgiven myself for that foolish lie. Mum tried to comfort me.

'He would have gone to sleep as soon as you left. Just remember all the treats you made him.'

'Yes, I know' I said. But I have never forgotten and it hurts me still.

We buried my father on a bitterly cold day in December. His grave was covered in a blanket of wreaths and flowers. In spite of the cold their perfume hung in the air. Dad was the first of Granny's sons to die. He was only sixty-three and everyone was shattered. My cousin Johnny came up to me. He started to speak but then stood shaking his head and tears rolled down his cheeks.

'I loved me Uncle Eddy,' he said and walked away. Those few words meant a lot to me.

There had been standing room only in the church and many more stood outside. My father had lived his life in the open air, enjoying the sun and the seasons. It was hard to realise that he would never experience these blessings again. We stood together at the graveside; one huge family. I tried to stop the tears but they came anyway.

'Don't cry Rosie,' said Aunt Britt, 'yer dad had a good life.'

It was true. He enjoyed every day and every day was a day to be lived to the full. My mother showed me the letters and cards she had received. Nearly every one mentioned his generosity and the huge enjoyment he had in hearing laughter and sharing a joke. My father was not perfect. Who is? Like all of us he had his faults. Standing by his grave I smiled as I remembered the childish arguments I had had with him. I can see him now, stamping off in a temper, not knowing for sure whether I was right or wrong and not knowing how to answer his eight-year-old daughter who thought she knew everything. I am very certain, though, that both my parents would have been proud of me and my books. They are a loving memorial to all of my extended family. That a Gypsy girl from Somerset could have books published is a dream come true.

6

A Posy of Wild Flowers

I well remember saying to a female teacher at my school, with all the confidence of a child who had never been put down by an adult, that I was going to be a teacher when I was 'growed up'. She gave me a sneering look and told me that first I should learn to speak correctly. Well, I may not have become a teacher but I have met many interesting people in my life. In my own way, I have been able to teach lots of things to different people who were able to learn because I understand how hard it is to learn anything if your teacher is impatient and he regards you as a 'dinlo' (an idiot). In fact, when I remember the times our teacher called us 'imbecile' or 'moron' or told us that we should be in the local madhouse, it makes me wonder how we poor cowering children learned anything. In that respect times have changed for the better. Children today believe that anything is possible for them and I admire their confidence, their abilities and their willingness to try. No child can usually excel at everything but each has their strengths and weaknesses.

I loved the written word. Poems were words that were strung together to form a delight to the ear. Essays were where I could let my imagination run riot; even spelling was a joy to me. I would study the way the letters formed a word. If I did this for too long the words seemed to lose all sense and I would quickly pass on. It was something I could enjoy at any time. I also loved being with people, talking to them and learning more about their lives. I could chat with a complete stranger for hours. I was out with my husband, John, one day. He was looking for bits and pieces for something he was working on.

'I saw you chatting away there,' he said. 'Who was that?'

'Oh, I don't know her,' I replied.

'How can you chat for ages with people you don't even know?'

I stared at him for a minute and then copied something my father did once. Spreading my arms wide, I said: 'Because I lo-o-o-ve them!' This love for people had grown from my upbringing and it formed the foundation of my new career.

When the children were all at school I worked in school meals to supplement our income. This fitted in well with school holidays and helped out with the children's clothes and shoes. I tried auxiliary nursing for a while on nights but eventually it was too much. So I found myself applying for the position of Home Help for Social Services. I was not sure it was for me but I applied anyway.

When I went for my interview I met with a very kind lady called Mrs Jordan. After passing every test I was told I could start at once and she would be my boss. I was to be given a rota of clients to visit who would be allocated from an hour to four hours a week depending on their need. Some would be disabled; most would be elderly.

I told myself I would only do it for six months. It seemed like such a great responsibility. I would have to make decisions without ringing the office constantly over every matter. Would I be able to do it? I wondered.

'Just remember,' Mrs Jordan advised, 'when you enter their front door, that it is their home and no matter how poor or how little they have, you must ask them first for permission to remove or throw anything away, no matter how insignificant it may seem to you.'

I forgot this golden rule the very first week. I threw away a piece of hard, mouldy cheese I had found nestling in the corner of a fridge, only to be told by a cross eighty-year-old lady that she had been going to make some cheese sandwiches for her tea. It was no use explaining to her that it was not fit to eat, so I ended up having to replace her cheese at my own expense.

'There!' she said, 'that may have looked bad to you, but I've had to eat many things that you may not have wanted to and I have been very glad to do so.'

She said this with an expression that said, 'you have no idea what I am talking about, do you?' But I did know. More than she realised. For a brief moment, I had forgotten how we had grown up on Granny's land, living on the things we grew from it and how hard our mother had tried to feed and clothe us. I saw it clearly, though, in the old lady's eyes.

Once I started meeting my clients, I was hooked. I fell in love with them. There were only one or two that were difficult. On the whole they were wonderful. I loved listening to their stories. I watched their faces as they remembered the days of their youth and my heart melted. I often held back tears of sorrow and sometimes laughter.

My very first client stands out in my memory, although I only went there for one morning to help her hang some curtains and put loose covers on her three-piece suite. She was waiting for me to arrive, standing expectantly in the open doorway.

'Hello!' she smiled, 'I'm so glad you've come nice and early. I've lots to do. We'll start on the bedrooms.'

The curtains, which had all been dry cleaned, were waiting on the beds. Every rug, cushion cover and bed-spread was a different colour and pattern. Florals fought with regency stripes, purples with oranges. My head began to ache.

'Aren't they beautiful?' she smiled as we began to hang her 'drapes' as she called them. They *were* very nice and if the rest of the room had been a plainer hue it would have all come together nicely. It did not take too long to hang three pairs of curtains. Each bedroom was very colourful to say the least.

'Now then,' she said firmly, 'we'll have a cuppa. Then we'll hang the lounge window. I can't wait for you to see them! When I was a girl, everything in my parents' house was a shade of brown or some other drab colour. I longed for some pretty things, but during and after the war, they just weren't in the shops unless you had the money for the black market! So, now I'm making up for lost time!'

She winked and whipped the lid off a large box with a dramatic flourish. 'Now, just look at these!'

I thought at first a mistake had been made and they had sent her a party dress instead. But no, she drew back the tissue paper and gently stroked the contents of the box. Shocking pink satin gleamed in the morning sunlight and cream lace frothed out of a smaller box. I could not believe my eyes.

'Curtains?' I questioned.

'Yes, yes,' she gloated, pressing the sensuous material to her bosom.

'So pretty! Just what I've always wanted.'

I looked around her lounge; every colour of the rainbow flashed before me and I tried to imagine what it would look like bedecked in shocking pink satin and cream lace. The window ran the length of the twenty-foot lounge and dropped from ceiling to floor. We placed kitchen chairs in front of it to support the excess fabric and then she produced a large bag of tiny curtain hooks that had to be painstakingly fixed before we could hang the curtains. I thought to myself that curtain rings would have been much easier and it brought to mind the great heavy wooden ones that I had played with as a child, threading them up my arms like bangles just as the air-raid siren went off and then being unable to stand and run to the shelter for the great weight of them. I wished I could have owned them still and I smiled as I pushed the fiddly little plastic hooks into the heading tape.

It was worth it to see a very happy woman standing before a glorious vision of pink satin and lace and completing our handiwork with several vases of beautiful roses of every hue, which strangely connected all the other colours in the room.

I was never sent to her again, but over the years, stories of the amazing window filtered back to me. I smiled as I remembered the curtains we had acquired in the camp during the war. Most people back then had some form of blackout curtains all through the war, so by the end of it everyone craved a bit of colour. A van had pulled up at our camp around this time while I was at school one day. My mother and a few aunts had pooled their money together and bought a large roll of bright salmon-pink corset satin from the man in the van. A pair of curtains for every wagon was sewed on Granny's old Singer sewing machine and by the end of the week every window in the camp was similarly adorned. My father's thoughts on the matter said it all.

'What a sight for sore eyes!' he commented. In time they faded to a more acceptable hue and then were finally replaced by my mother with fresh blue and white gingham, which was easier on the eye.

In the first week in my new job, most of the people I had been sent to only needed the odd morning and this got me into the swing of things. By the end of the week I had received the names and addresses of my future permanent clients. I was not at all nervous. I liked people and hoped that they would all like me. However, I was in for a shock.

I knocked at the door of a large house with an overgrown garden. I knew that this house had stood empty for years and now twin sisters lived there. The door flew open suddenly.

'Who be you then?'

I looked up. I had to – I'm five-foot-one and the very large lady towering above me was at least eleven inches taller than me.

'I'm your new home help,' I said softly, 'I've come to help you twice a week for four hours total.'

'Nah, nah,' she said looking me over like a slightly smelly joint of beef, 'You'm no good to me. You'm too smart. I wants a gal who can work, not one who's afraid to get 'er 'ands wet!'

Well, I thought, that's put me in my place. In an effort to look as decent as possible and bearing in mind I would have to work, I had put on a four-year-old Marks and Spencer's cotton suit and two-year-old sandals. Even I could not believe that I looked like a fashion plate. Yet this huge person in her down-at-heel slippers and an old frock that had seen better days obviously thought so. She made as if to close the door.

'Nah, I needs a gal that don't mind work!'

'Please wait,' I said, 'Give me a chance. I've got my overall in my bag. And my rubber gloves.'

She looked down her nose at me as if making a

decision she knew she would regret and backed down.

'All right,' she said grudgingly, 'I'll see 'ow you pans out.'

So I, in all my fashionable glory, stepped inside the smelliest house I had ever been in. That was the real start of more than two decades of service to others.

'I'll let me sister 'ave a look at you,' she said, showing me into a pretty bedroom. In a tiny armchair sat an equally tiny, white-haired old lady. What a contrast. In my mind I called her 'little twin' and her sister 'big twin'.

'Come here, dear,' she beckoned sweetly, 'bend down.'

I did so, thinking she may have been deaf. Then she grabbed hold of a chunk of my hair, which I wore in a shiny bob.

'Ouch!' I shouted, 'Stop that!'

She let go. My eyes were full of tears of pain. I turned to speak to big twin and caught her hiding a sly grin. I stood up to confront her.

'This won't do,' I said. 'You will not be allowed help if you abuse those of us who are sent to you. If it happens again, I'll report it.'

'I expect she thought it was a wig,' said big twin ruefully.

I shot little twin a glance and marched to the door.

'Right. Where do you want me to start?'

'In the kitchen, please,' said big twin, staring at me with respect.

The kitchen was full of old cupboards. 'Chuck these out and do what you kin with the floor.'

Perhaps I should have turned up with a wraparound pinny, my hair in a turban and a fag stuck to my bottom lip, I smiled to myself. I set to work, moving the old cupboards out into the garden. Then, to my horror, what seemed like hundreds of mice were scurrying around the kitchen. I was to see this sort of thing over and over again. Every home I visited in this small village had at least one mouse and many were infested. Everyone seemed to tolerate these little creatures but I had never seen so many in one place. Although I had been brought up with a love of nature, vermin were an exception. Big twin started screeching.

'Kill 'em! Kill 'em!'

'No!' I screeched back, 'I can't kill 'em!'

Grabbing a broom, I swept as many as I could into the overgrown garden. I turned to big twin, who was brandishing her stick and pointing at the larder. A tiny, terrified mouse was cowering in the corner as if frozen to the spot.

'Kill it! Kill it!' she yelled. I refused and swept it outside to join its mates.

'I'll do what I can,' I said, 'if you just leave me to it.'

Big twin sat on a chair in the hall watching me and saying nothing. I threw all the broken furniture into the garden and poured buckets of boiling soda water over the beautiful red tiles, scrubbing them hard with a stiff broom. I remembered my Granny treating her rugs to the same method of cleaning as I coveted that beautiful floor. When I had finished for the day, I spread the table with a lovely white cloth and put the kettle on the Aga. Even I was amazed at how fresh and pretty everything looked.

'Stay fer a cuppa,' big twin offered.

'Not today thanks. I'm in a bit of a hurry,' I smiled, thinking to myself how glad I was that I had witnessed her wiping out little twin's potty with her tea towel. I intended to stop that filthy habit. If I was allowed to stay that is.

'Well?' I said, picking up my bag, 'am I to stay or am I to go?'

'What d'you mean?' big twin laughed. 'Why, when I seed you chuckin' down that b'ilin' water over that greasy floor, I nearly stood up an' shouted the 'alley-looyah chorus! I thought, yes, this is the gal fer me. She'll do. I want no other.'

I stayed with the twins for five years and enjoyed every minute. They lived to ninety-six or seven. I still visited them when they moved nearer to their family.

'Look,' they would say to visitors, 'this is our gal Rosie. Don't she look lovely? Proper little fashion plate she is but we don't 'old it agin 'er. She's a worker she is.' Then they would recite the story of my first day and their amazement when I chucked buckets of b'ilin' water over their red tiled floor even though I was dressed to the nines.

7

Fool's Parsley

Living in a seaside town and not far from the countryside, I found it very pleasant to walk to and from my clients' homes. They all lived in fairly close proximity to each other. John often drove me to work or picked me up if the weather was bad, but I really preferred the walk. There was so much to see on the way.

I often used the public footpaths as a short cut. One very dear lady, Mrs P, was a lover of all wild things so I would regularly pick her a bouquet of wild flowers framed with Queen Anne's Lace and tied with a strand of grass. Her face would light up at this natural posy.

'Oh, thank you! How lovely!' she would say. 'Please get me my crystal vase.'

She would sniff at them deeply and then arrange them to place in the centre of her table where they looked beautiful. She knew lots of little sayings and so did I, so we were always playfully trying to outdo each other. I used to tell her little stories from my childhood and she would tell me some of hers. When my cousins and I were very young we never killed insects or any living thing. However, Mrs P would say, 'Please clean the windows in the extension – and don't leave any spiders, or their nests! I don't like creepy crawlies!'

'But they work so hard to make their home and lay their eggs. It seems so cruel to destroy all their hard work,' I would reply. She despaired of me when, instead of killing the snails, I would carefully remove them to a place where they would be safe, elsewhere in her garden. She could not believe her eyes when she asked me to put a plant in her garden and I accidentally dug up an ants' nest and carefully replaced the earth to its original state. I was devastated to see all the parent ants hurrying to save their eggs after being so rudely disturbed. Later on I overheard her telling a visitor about it.

'You should see my home help washing around the spiders and saving the snails. She will *not* get rid of them. Last year she saved an ants' nest! They must have thought, "this is a nice safe house" because this house was full of them all the summer!'

Then she added that I was a wonderful worker and we got on ever so well.

I could never really describe to her the simple pleasure we got as children from watching a spider spin its web until it was complete, or marvelling at the webs hanging from the clothes line on a frosty autumn morning, a huge spider hanging like a jewel in the centre surrounded by frosty 'diamonds'. We had hours of enjoyment looking at the snails carrying their homes on their backs, gently touching their little 'horns' and watching them first withdraw and then, when it was safe, pop out again. 'Why are their 'ouses so little?' Teddy, my little brother, asked one day. 'If it was a bit bigger, 'e could go right in and look out of 'is little window, like our wagon!'

We had all thought that was very funny and I still think of it whenever I see a snail.

Mrs P never knew I was a Gypsy, or if she guessed she said nothing. I personally had endless amusement when she would comment on my Aunt Amy, who 'told fortunes' in town.

'I got Amy, the Gypsy, to tell me my fortune today,' she said. 'She told me I would never sell my house or leave this part of the world. What do you think?'

'No Mrs P, I don't think you will leave either,' I smiled.

My reasoning being that her house had so much stuff in it that she would not know where to begin. Her home was crammed full of things she had been buying and 'collecting' for sixty years or more. Cleaning her house was like working with a jigsaw puzzle: moving a small pile of clothes here or a heavy chair there and just cleaning that bit, then putting them back and repeating the process somewhere else.

It is very strange how things that happen in your childhood repeat themselves in later life. One of the teachers came to our school for just two weeks to cover for someone who was sick. She taught Nature Study and to me did not look the part at all. She certainly looked nothing like the teacher she had replaced. She was young and very elegant and her clothes were beautiful, unlike our other teachers who wore the same clothes day in and day out. She had a different outfit for every day. She had a very pretty face and her hair was Marcel waved. Definitely out of the 'top drawer', as my mother would have said. She arrived at the school in a pretty little sports car and smoked her cigarette in a long black and white cigarette holder, no doubt causing a bit of jealousy among the female teachers, judging by the sidelong looks they gave her. We soon learned that she was extremely superstitious and everything she saw was either lucky or unlucky. She was very likeable even though some of the things she believed were quite foolish. So when I was sent to an elderly lady who could have been an older version of her in that respect, I was quite pleased, thinking she would have the same sunny disposition as the young woman I had known so long ago. This was not so, however, and the old lady became the bane of everyone's lives amongst those who knew her.

'Good morning, Miss Freda. How are you?' I said cheerily.

'Close the door quickly, I don't want to see all that green, it's unlucky!' she said when I came to her home for the very first time.

'What do you mean?' I asked.

'There, out there!' she said, pointing a long bony finger at the large patch of grass the children played on. I was perplexed.

'But grass is everywhere!'

'Yes, I know, but I don't want to see it. I cut it out of my mind.'

How she did this I do not know. I found her to be an interesting person and amusing, especially when she did not intend to be. She was a complete hypochondriac and every day I had to listen to her symptoms.

'Oh, my dear!' she would cry as I walked in the door, 'my brain tumour is bad today. My head, oh my poor head!'

She would lean back in her chair, languidly touching the back of her hand against her forehead.

'It can't be a brain tumour or you would have died years ago.'

Apparently she had first had symptoms when she was twelve. I realised I had been a little harsh when she hardly spoke to me all morning. I soon learned that she liked to be taken seriously. No matter how hot the day was, she would not open any windows. Summer or winter, she would keep the gas fire burning all day. Having been brought up in the open air, this was something I could not bear. One particularly hot day, a blast of hotter air hit me as I walked into her living room.

'Please, can we have the fire off and open a window? It's like an oven in here!' I gasped.

'No, the bugs will come in!' she insisted. Perspiration ran down my face and neck as I threw open all the windows.

'The bugs! The bugs!' she cried.

'I can't help it, it's the bugs or me!' I puffed, hanging out of the window gasping for air. She spoke to me a little stiffly after that so I gently suggested that maybe

I could ask my boss if she could send someone else. At that she burst into tears.

'Please, don't leave!'

'Don't worry, you will not be left with no one at all. Perhaps,' I added wryly, 'you will be sent someone who doesn't mind being hot!'

No, she wanted me. Now, this lady would not use a public telephone box under any circumstances (because of the bugs) and yet she had not had a telephone installed in her home either. Not that many people did in the 1970s. Yet that evening she telephoned me four or five times from the public telephone box at the end of her road (across the patch of green grass) to beg me not to leave. I realised how upset she was at the thought.

'Go home; make yourself a hot drink and go to bed, Miss Freda. I promise I won't leave.' I said reassuringly.

'Oh, thank you so much!' she sighed.

After that, she was not perfect but she did try very hard to be more reasonable and gradually I grew to like her and her funny ways very much indeed.

Someone had told her many years ago that dragon-flies could give you 'quite a dreadful sting, my dear' and ladybirds would bite you if you were wearing anything floral.

She was an only child, much loved by Mummy and Daddy, by her account, but apparently even Daddy couldn't put up with his daughter's hypochondria. One night she arrived home convinced she had yet another dreadful illness. She searched everywhere for her 'Medical Diagnosis' book so she could consult it to make sure she was not dying. She could not find it anywhere. In the end, her father confessed that he had burned it as he was sick and tired of her many illnesses and hoped that would be the end of it. Unfortunately not, as she went and bought another that was twice as big with dozens of really interesting diseases in it. She owned it still and many times I would find her at her kitchen table trying to discover if her new lump or pain was serious or not.

I dropped in on my mother on the way home and told her all about my new client. Mum was a trustworthy confidante. She laughed and gasped in all the right places.

'Do you recall that old Romany gentleman who used to ride his horse around the nearby villages when you were small, Rosie? He used to crack his whip and shouted at anyone who looked at him or who he thought was talking about him!'

'Oh, yes, I remember him!' I laughed, 'I do remember Dad warning us that whatever happened we must never look him in the eye and never ever call him a "Dinlo".'

We asked him why not but Dad just said 'never do it or else'. We soon forgot his words of admonition until one Friday afternoon when we all streamed out of school to the bus stop. The old Romany gentleman was riding by and as a rule we took no notice of him, but someone (I do not know who) suddenly shouted 'Dinlo! Dinlo!' His head came up and, raising his whip, he snarled at us.

'Who called I a Dinlo?' he demanded.

Instead of waiting for the bus, we ran for home as one body, shrieking with fright. The old man followed at our heels, snapping his whip behind us, which made us run even faster. He chased us right to the camp gate, where we arrived breathless and blubbing. He slowly dismounted and walked his horse into our yard. Everyone who was home came out to see what the fuss was all about. Dad and my uncles were on top of a lorry load of scrap and they looked up when they heard the old man shout to them.

'These wicked chavvies called me a "Dinlo!"' he growled. We all protested our innocence but had to say sorry to the old gentleman. He nodded his head and grunted by way of acknowledgement and Granny gave him a cup of tea with a tot of whisky to calm him down. After he left, we all got a dressing down and my father explained that the old chap had a mental illness but that he was harmless.

'He didn't seem very harmless to me!' I said. 'If that there whip would've touched us, we could've been very hurted!'

'That goes t' show that far from being a Dinlo, 'e was a very clever man!' said Dad, ''E knew just 'ow far 'e could crack 'is whip and not touch any of 'ee! I knew 'im when 'e used t' be a champion with that whip! 'E could whip a lighted cigarette from a man's lips afore ye could say "knife". If 'e 'ad *wanted* t' 'arm any of 'ee, 'e could've done it. 'E didn't want t' 'arm 'ee, so 'e didn't.'

I came back to the present.

'I don't think I want to see any more people with strange ways,' I said.

My mother looked at me sideways.

'The trouble with you, Rosie, is that you draw people out. Deep down, you need to know all their ways and all their secrets. When you were a little girl you were always in the middle of any goings on. Now you're in a position to hear everyone's secrets and you have to keep them to yourself.'

'Well I don't mind that. I can do that, it's just that sometimes enough is enough.'

Miss Freda never married, which did not surprise me. She had got engaged though and she had been given a really beautiful diamond ring from her suitor, but the engagement was broken off apparently.

'Did you return the ring?' I asked.

'Certainly not!' she replied, curling her lip. 'I sold it and bought a bike. Far more sensible. Had it for years. Much better than a husband!'

Looking at her, I knew it was better that she had not married. If her own father could not put up with her hypochondria, a husband would have had no chance.

She was very much a lady, but on occasions she could be quite uncouth. I had to accompany her once to a posh restaurant with several of her friends. They sat around the table looking like a picture postcard of 1930s ladies having tea at the Ritz. Just as the waiter replenished her glass of water she gave a huge belch.

'Bugger the beer!' she said, patting her belly.

I thought how my Granny would have loved to have met her and shown her how to make her own cures with all the herbs to be found in the countryside.

When she was seventy-six she went into a nursing home some distance away. She died shortly after and left me a china ornament of a little laughing dog, which

I have always loved. It had been a present to her from the young man to whom she had been engaged and although she had often told me she didn't like 'the ugly thing' she had kept it all those years. I still have it and it reminds me of her even now.

Something I did come across time and time again was a kind of unthinking prejudice even from those who were kind in other respects. I had been sent my instructions for a new client. I walked up a long drive to a lovely house set into a huge garden with what looked like a large orchard full of fruit trees at the rear. The side garden grew raspberry canes as well as blackcurrant and gooseberry bushes. I also noticed several rows of strawberries. I was looking forward to working here. I had no answer from the front door so I followed the path to the back door. Suddenly, I heard shouting and banging.

'Get out of that there garden yer dirty beast! Get out! Get out!'

More bangs and crashes followed. I heard a cry of anger so I hurried round to see what was going on. I half thought it might be the woman's husband but there had been no mention of it on the worksheet. I rounded the corner of the house just in time to be almost knocked over by a huge Billy goat! Never stopping to see if I was all right, my client pushed the goat out of a gate in the hedge and locked it behind him. She turned to me, wiping her brow and smoothing down her clothes.

'Who be you then gal?' she asked, trying to get her hair tidied back into its bun. I introduced myself and explained that Social Services had sent me to help her for a couple of hours twice a week if that suited her.

'Tell yer the truth my gal, I could do with somebody every day. I got plenty to do!'

'Sorry,' I said, 'that's all the time I can give you.'

'Come on in then. Let's get started.'

I followed her into her kitchen. I thought I had seen everything but I was shocked to the core. Dogs, cats and chickens were everywhere. On the table and on the cooker, on the vegetable rack and on the windowsill. I managed to keep the look of shock off my face.

'Take yer coat off and hang it up,' she said. She did not say where so I hooked it over a broom handle which was beside a cupboard, and I placed my bag on the floor. At once, three hens began pecking inside so I quickly removed it. There did not seem to be anywhere else to put it out of their way so I held onto it. I turned to my new lady. She had a large pinny wrapped around her large body and down-at-heel slippers, which fell off with almost every step she took. Her hair was trying to stay put in an untidy bun and spectacles were perched on the end of her turned-up nose. I thought she looked as though she was going to take off.

'I'm sorry gal,' she apologised, 'I got up early to get a bit sorted but I had to go down to me bottom orchard. They blasted Gyppos got thereselves into it. I bin down there 'smornin' to tell 'em to go. I bet I won't have an egg left if they stays. Then the blasted goat got out!'

Well, I thought. This is a fine start! I looked her in the eye.

'Well, maybe "they blasted Gyppos" will give you a

hand to get some of your fruit picked,' I said wryly. 'I've heard "they blasted Gyppos" are good at fruit and vegetable picking. It earns them a bit of money.'

'Yes but it'll be one fer me and two fer they!'

'What do you usually do with it all? It's a very large orchard.'

'A lot of it rots on the trees, the crows has a few and the rest drops.'

'That attracts the wasps though. It would be better to give it away than waste it surely?'

'I'll think about it.'

Mrs Jones needed a lot to be done. Going upstairs had become difficult so she needed help to move her bedroom downstairs to an unused dining room. She had a downstairs bathroom, which made things a lot easier. We slowly got cleared up downstairs and we arranged for someone to take the spare furniture upstairs. She was well pleased when it was finished. It was a very large house with several bedrooms. When we came to sort out her living room we found six room-sized rugs behind the sofa.

'We can move them on our own,' she said. 'They can go upstairs.'

I was a bit doubtful. I could see they were heavy and there was no one else around to help. After tidying everything else we tried to get the rugs upstairs but we only just managed to drag one to the bottom. We tried our best but had to give up. They were old rugs but quite valuable and she did not want to part with them.

'Never mind,' she said airily, 'we'll just have to put them in the old morning room. I don't use it no more.'

The morning room door opened on the other side of the stairs and was level, but it still took us over an hour to move them. The rugs were all rolled up so we decided we would put them against the far wall out of the way. After dragging the first one over, we soon realised that the rugs were longer than the room was wide.

'Oh no, my dear gal,' she panted, the sweat pouring down her face which was very grubby by now. 'We can't give up now or I will fall over 'em and break me leg or me hip!'

It was well past my home time but I dared not leave her in this muddle. The more I looked at the rugs, the more I realised that there was only one solution; we would have to pile them in the middle of the room. We could just fit them in, as there was a large bay window at the front. She agreed. When we had finished we were both exhausted and sat down on the large pile. To my dismay, we then realised that we could not close the door as the rug on the bottom of the pile was in the way. We stood in the hall gazing at the mountain of rugs wondering what to do. Mrs Jones suddenly clapped her hands.

'Oh well,' she said triumphantly, 'no one will notice they, will they?'

I looked at her and she looked at me and I gave a sudden snort. Then we were holding our stomachs and laughing like no one has laughed before. To think that no one would notice a huge pile of carpets and they would somehow be rendered invisible was more than we could bear.

I continued to be Mrs Jones's home help for nearly

two years and the carpets stayed in the middle of the room all that time. I truly believe that they did become invisible to her, but never to me. When the house eventually went up for sale, I helped her to pack the things she wanted to keep and throw out the things she did not want. There were a lot of items in that big house and it was tiring work. We sat on packing cases drinking a cup of tea.

'We're nearly finished now. What are you going to do with all those huge carpets? We'll never be able to move them on our own.'

She stared at me owlishly through her spectacles.

'What carpets?'

I remembered Granny and Granfer and the carpets and rugs Granfer brought home from his trips to the market. I thought how they would have laughed to hear about Mrs Jones. Some of the rugs Granfer brought back were very valuable, although he said he bought them 'fer a song'. None of that worried Granny. Colour, size or thickness made no difference. She never measured them. If she needed a new carpet for her hut she would just take out the sofa, lay the rug on the floor, pick up a sharp knife and cut the rug around the cupboard or whatever was in the way. When she had finished she would be well pleased. On top of this she would throw a few more rugs and replace the sofa. That was that for a few weeks until Granny decided that the new rugs needed a good scrub. She would take them all outside onto the concrete in the yard over the runaway from the wash-house, which took the dirty water from the wash-house down to the ditch. She scrubbed away with hot soapy water and a stiff broom and then rinsed it all with several buckets of cold water. She then spread them over the hedges in the hot sun until they were dry. Of course, most of the bright colours had been all washed away, but never mind; all was clean again and that was good enough for Granny. The value to her was in the usefulness of them. They served their purpose as a covering for the floor. Granny fought a losing battle because every one of us grandchildren, my aunts and uncles and the dogs were in and out all day. The fact that the yard was coated in a thick, black, composted layer of rust, earth and wasted oil from the scrap did not help either. She must have got fed up with us bringing in dirt and muck with us all the time. We did not think of all the work we must have made for her but I have often thought of it since.

8

Meadow Sweet

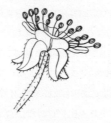

When Granny bought her 'bit o' ground' she spent nearly every penny she had and had no idea where the next would come from. Nothing daunted, she would pack her basket with everything saleable she had, even going so far as to pick a few bunches of wild flowers from the grassy verge, and then went out hawking from door to door until it was all sold. Granny must have been in her thirties then, when I was a little girl, but she always seemed old to me. She had a very insistent personality, so I imagine not many could go past her without buying a little something. When she came home, her basket was full of groceries – a day's work well done. That was how Granny worked from the day she moved onto her bit of ground until the day she died. Granny thought we would all be safe there and that no one would ever be able to move us on. It was her insurance and our inheritance for as long as we needed it. She was astonished when some tried, however.

'This yer is moi grownd!' she told the men from the council. 'I ain't worryin' thee, so don't 'ee worry about I! I paid cash for this bit o' grownd. Nobuddy give it me, least of all 'ee. I ain't asked you lot fer anythin'.'

'But madam,' the gentleman replied politely, 'if we let every Tom Dick or Harry have it their own way, we would be in a right old mess.'

'Leave we alone,' said Granny, 'we bin all right without 'ee 'elpin'. Just leave me be.'

She pointed at his car parked in our yard and he left. He returned many times, sometimes with other men from the council, sometimes with sheets of paper which Granny could not read and was too 'deaf' to hear read out. Granny believed it was only the tea laced with whisky that they came for, but whatever the reason, Granny was eventually left in peace. No more letters came from the council so Granny planted trees and dozens of rose bushes all around the inner boundaries of her ground. They were a glorious sight all through the summer and we would go to sleep with their heavy perfume and wake up with the same wonderful scented air.

No wonder we all grew up with a love of nature and gardening in our blood. Even now Gypsies are not allowed to do as they please with their own land and they find this very difficult to understand. Of course we all have to obey the laws of the land but an Englishman's home is no longer his 'castle' and a Gypsy cannot site his wagon anywhere he wants to for the night or put it on his own land either. The dilemma continues.

I could never understand why Gypsies are called

'dirty'. In my life I have met many people who lived in houses, some of which were clean and some of which were filthy. I have seen caravans at the side of the road surrounded by rubbish and dogs running loose and I have seen sparkling caravans on the green with patio sets outside. Three days later when passing they had moved on. You would not have known anyone had been there, as not so much as a speck of rubbish was to be seen. Whether or not the inhabitants were Gypsies, travellers or some other group I do not know. Everyone is an individual.

I remembered how much my mother had loved her garden. Gypsies have a great love for bright colours and seeing them grow in the natural patterns and colours God intended was always a great joy. My mother's garden at the camp was not huge but it was very fertile. Part of it was where an old chicken run had been. She truly had green fingers. If she stuck a twig in, she would have a little tree growing in no time at all. Her strawberries and raspberries tasted like no others I have eaten in the years since her death and sometimes I buy soft fruit in the hope of being surprised by the wonderful taste, but so far I have been disappointed.

'Rosie,' she said, one spring day, 'I'm going to plant a special apple tree. It will only be as tall as me; four feet six inches. It will even have apples in the first year – my favourite – Cox's Orange Pippin!'

She planted her tree and we watched it thrive and blossom. Mum was so thrilled. Every time I took my four children to see her, she would proudly show us how well her tree was growing.

Claire, my youngest and one of the twins, was about four and a half years old at the time. We regularly visited on a Sunday teatime and one day Claire wandered off down the garden. It was almost the end of the summer holidays and the twins were due to start school soon.

'How are your apples doing, Mum?' I asked.

Before she could reply, Claire climbed up the caravan steps, her face all smiles.

'Look, Granny!' she said excitedly, holding out her skirt hem, 'I've picked all of your apples for you!'

In the folds of her dress were seven or eight marble-sized green apples. The little girl's delighted face was in total conflict with the dismay on my mother's and she could not hide it. Immediately seeing this, Claire's eyes brimmed with tears. That made two tearful faces. Then Mum knelt and put her arms around her little granddaughter.

'It's a bit too soon to pick them yet, Claire, and we won't be able to eat them as they're too small. They will be bigger next year and then we can pick them together.'

Claire's face brightened.

'Yes! Yes, Granny!' And that is what they did.

During the years I worked as a home help for Social Services, I saw many beautiful gardens. There was one married couple I went to for just a short time. The husband was a wonderful man but his wife was the complete opposite. While he waited on her hand and foot and adored her completely, she was always complaining about her health and him in equal measure. She lay in bed most days, although she didn't have any serious medical problems.

After a few short weeks, I had knocked on the front door as usual and rung the bell, but there was no answer. When I walked around the back I discovered the poor old man lying on the kitchen floor. He had suffered a heart attack. His wife's breakfast tray was on the table, ready to take upstairs, and the kettle was boiling away for morning tea. He would never take his wife breakfast in bed again.

After his death, his wife tried to apply for some extra help from Social Services, but this was refused. She was forced to muddle along and do more for herself. In the end she decided to sell up.

I arrived one morning to her request to open her husband's greenhouse so she could get me to clear it out. I refused, as it was one of the jobs we were not supposed to do. However, when we opened up the greenhouse I could see how busy this poor man had been up until his death. There were hundreds of geranium cuttings in little pots ready to plant out. His greenhouse and garden had obviously been his pride and joy.

'Just chuck the plants out, then!' she said. I stared at her.

'What? After all your husband's hard work? It seems such a shame!'

The old lady just shrugged. I know I shouldn't have but I said impulsively, 'I'll plant them for him then.'

Of course, she agreed. I spent the rest of the morning planting beds of geraniums and watering them in as I had seen my mother do to make sure they 'took'. Happily we had a few days of warm showers so they did well. A few weeks later I was sent somewhere else but eventually was sent to one of her neighbours. I was amazed to see that all the geraniums were in full bloom and a riot of colours. I remarked to my client on how lovely the garden looked.

'Yes,' she said. 'She sold her house because the buyer thought the garden looked so lovely. A few weeks ago it was even better than it is now. She told us how hard she worked, planting in memory of her husband.'

I said nothing. What was the point? I never saw her again.

One of my clients had had an operation on her thyroid, which left her with a strange side effect – extremely rapid speech. When I first went to her I found her very difficult to understand, but in time I managed to filter out the important from the unimportant. Her name was Mrs Merrie and she was another wonderful gardener; her garden bloomed all the year round. She gave me lots of plants and fruit trees she had grown herself and although she employed a gardener she was always coaxing someone or other to help her. One of the rules I had to keep to was that we were only supposed to do shopping and housework, yet I knew many of us home helps did some gardening, including me. I never minded helping Mrs Merrie, though, as the peace I felt in her garden was unbelievable. I often thought of taking up a job gardening but then when it was cold and wet I was glad to be indoors.

Mrs Merrie was in her nineties when I first met her. She opened her door after several knocks, chatting away nineteen to the dozen.

'Come in and see what I look like in my new coat!' she said. The living room was littered with sewing things.

'Help me put my coat on, dear.'

She handed me a heavy tweed coat with a full swing back. It was of a good quality. I helped her put it on and she turned this way and that. It looked very good on her and expensive. Then she took it off and showed me the miracle she had performed. She explained:

'See what I did first? I couldn't afford a new coat of this quality, so I unpicked my old winter coat and turned it inside out and then replaced the lining! The material was still good inside.'

The coat was at least twenty years old, she told me, but the inside was not faded or worn at all.

'With a new belt and buttons it's as good as new!'

I gazed at this beautiful garment in amazement, wondering how these bony fingers had created such a masterpiece. Even as a non-sewer I could see the hours of work that had gone into this labour of love.

'Well!' I said, 'I would never have known that this was a makeover if you hadn't have told me. What a clever lady you are!'

Mrs Merrie's home was full of beautiful things she had made herself but I especially admired a pair of cream wool rugs she had made for her bedroom. They almost covered the floor and were so heavy it took two of us to lift and shake them. She was always busy doing something but I really fell for her way of getting me to do things I was not supposed to, probably because I knew she was so industrious despite her age.

One day I arrived as usual at nine in the morning and knocked several times but with no answer. I walked around the back. To my utter shock, I was greeted by the sight of a ninety-year-old lady halfway up a ladder with a large brush in one hand and a pot of paint in the other. I managed to stop myself from crying out and went up to the ladder, speaking as quietly and as calmly as I could.

'Mrs Merrie, what are you doing up this ladder? Please come down at once.'

'Oh, my dear, I cannot leave this job another minute. I'll do this while you vacuum round,' she casually replied.

'No, come down.' She took no notice whatsoever.

'I'll get into trouble if you don't,' I tried. She heaved a sigh.

'Oh dear, why can't I paint my own wall?'

Somehow (I do not know quite how it happened), I found myself draped in an old brown mac with a peaked cap covering my hair and halfway up a ladder. In the two hours I was allocated I painted half the wall and completed the job on my next home visit. I tried to tell her that if it came out that I had painted her house on a ladder I would lose my job, as I was not supposed to do anything dangerous. No, she could not see my point.

'Why can't you do jobs outside? I don't see why not. I can't do it all.'

'Well, for a start, I'm obviously saving you a lot of money doing painting and decorating, Mrs Merrie – not to mention gardening. It's heavy work and I'm not insured for it.'

No more was said on the subject but I decided to ask to be moved to someone else if possible. Shortly after I was moved and we parted on friendly terms.

A few weeks later I stepped off the bus in the same road. Surely that was paint I could smell? I turned the corner and to my right, muffled in an old brown mac and a man's cap, halfway up a ladder was a colleague I knew by sight. She saw me at the same time as I spotted her. Bending her shoulders and turning away in an effort to disguise herself, she lost her grip on the paint tin. I walked on laughing to myself, although it must have taken hours to clean up the mess. I hoped common sense would prevail but I noticed the bungalow newly painted sometime later, though the ends never were.

I saved up all my funny stories to tell my mother. When Mum and I finished laughing about it she said she remembered Granny and her annual paint ritual.

'Yes, I feel sad to think of all the beautiful pieces of furniture she painted brown, improving them no end in her eyes. Granny would have loved Mrs Merrie's garden. She was a woman after her own heart.'

'Why *did* Granny paint everything brown?' I asked.

'It would have been a crime to throw away paint, so she mixed it all together to save money and it was used for all sorts of purposes. Colour didn't come into it,' she replied.

This dark-coloured paint would be used on chicken runs, garden sheds and fences as well. Many of my clients were from that era and I went into many a home where there was a cupboard or drawer crammed with anything reusable: string, brown paper, pins, elastic. In those days recycling was down to a fine art. Granny would not have had cream wool rugs though.

When John recently repainted the shed he used several pots of leftover paint and made a very nice dark blue. There was not quite enough for the back, so as it was not on show he said, 'I'll paint that when I get a spare bit of paint.' He was pleased with the result.

'That saved me ten or twenty pounds, I reckon,' he said, standing back to admire his resourcefulness. I thought to myself, 'He's doing a Granny,' and I told him so. That was a great compliment, as he knew how hard she had always worked. In fact, I believe he has all of Granny's saving ways. If any of our grandsons ever need a tool or anything useful and they ask him if they can borrow it, nine times out of ten he will search through his boxes of what I call 'junk' and, with an 'I'm very clever' look, hand it over. This includes many handmade tools, which he crafted because he could not find something he needed. Yes, Granny would have admired John for saving us a lot by repairing things himself.

9

Brambles

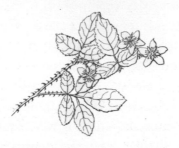

After my father died, as a family we were always there for my mother. She still lived in her blue caravan for many years afterwards at the camp. We all rallied round and visited often. If she needed us urgently she only had to phone. Aunt Betsy still lived in her little hut near the gate, spending her days feeding the men mugs of tea and stew while they worked on the scrap metal. She would go and check on Mum every morning. Mum would always have the caravan door open and Betsy would poke her blonde, French-pleated head around it.

'Morning Mary! You be all right?'

'Yes, thank you Betsy,' Mum would reply, usually with a bowl of cereal in her hand.

'What's that you be eatin' there, then?'

'Muesli, Betsy.'

'You don't wanna be eatin' all they nuts and stuff! I'll bring you some proper grub.' So saying she whipped the bowl of expensive muesli from my mother's grasp and scattered it for the birds. Mum was lost for words. Betsy was back shortly with a fry-up that would beat any full-grown man, enough for three or four people.

'There!' Betsy said, proudly. 'Get that down you. Do you good!'

Poor Mum tried her best but she was a tiny thing. She never ate fried food and the amount itself was enough to put her off. She knew Betsy meant well but she did not know how to tell her without hurting her feelings.

'Rosie,' she confided in me one day, 'can you tell Betsy that the doctor has told me not to eat fried food?'

'Yes,' I agreed. 'She just wants to make sure you're well looked after.'

'Yes, but look at this!' Mum exclaimed, opening her little fridge. 'This is what's left from the Sunday roast she gave me!'

I had to smile. There were four or five large slices of meat, half a dozen roast potatoes and three or four types of vegetables left over. It would almost have been enough to feed my family. I decided to pop in on Betsy before I left. She had the kettle on before I got to her door.

'Aunt Betsy,' I began over a cuppa, 'Mum has been telling me how well you've been looking after her. The only thing is, her doctor has told her not to eat so much food. It all looks delicious, but a quarter of the amount would be more than enough. You know how she hates any sort of waste.'

Aunt Betsy nodded. I continued, carefully.

'Mum's got a lot of time on her hands now Dad has died. She needs something to do with her days. She can't even do any gardening at the moment because it's so cold. Cooking helps her to pass the time.'

'Well, they old nuts and dried up currants ain't gonna do 'er no good!' she growled.

'That's muesli. The doctor says Mum needs to eat it. It's good for you. Fried food tastes good, but it's not very good for your heart.'

'Well, look at me! A spoon full o' best olive oil every mornin' does yer good!'

I could not argue with this. At the time Aunt Betsy was in her eighties but even in a bright light could have passed for fifty. Her skin, hair and teeth were perfect. We used to laugh at her olive oil mantra when we were younger but time proved her right. She was in her late nineties when she died, still taking her daily dose of olive oil.

We were always grateful for her help and Mum helped Aunt Betsy in return if she needed it. She helped her out with reading letters and filling in forms often. My cousins Carol and Henry were still living in the camp, too, and were there for both of them. What a wonderful example they set. In my work I have watched many lonely old people leave their own homes and go into residential care homes. When I went to visit them in their new residences I saw poor old souls, who only a few short weeks before had been looking after themselves to a degree, behaving like very young children, dependent for every need and with no life left in them. Many times in my working day I saw the same thing.

What was missing from so many lives was exactly what we had been brought up so rich in, a sense of family and community.

I had been given new clients, a disabled married couple. He had had his leg amputated, so Mrs Jordan briefed me on their needs and explained that he could be very difficult and sometimes aggressive. I had been warned. I arrived at their home with apprehension. He opened the door to me in his wheelchair.

'Good morning! I'm Rosemary, your home help.'

'I hope you've wiped your feet!' he grumbled.

'I have,' I said. 'My mother always taught me my manners.'

He glared at me but kept quiet. Elvis Presley was singing in the background about his blue, blue, blue suede shoes. I followed him into the kitchen.

'Nice song,' I said. He ignored me so I asked him to turn the radio down a bit in case he was hard of hearing. After a few minutes he did as I asked. I turned to his wife, who sat quietly on a kitchen chair.

'What would you like me to do for you today?'

She just glared at me too. Well, I thought, I'm nipping this behaviour in the bud. I had work to do. I calmly sat down, picked up the paper that he had been reading, put my feet up on the footstool and pretended to read. After a few minutes he finally spoke up.

'Do your job missus!'

'What job would that be then?' I asked expectantly.

'You should know,' he grunted.

'Well I'm here to help but unless you give me a clue, how would I know?'

After more blank looks from the pair of them, I tried again.

'What did your last home help do?'

'Very little,' he growled.

'Well, it all looks very clean. She must have worked hard ... unless you are able to help yourselves?'

'No, of course we can't do housework!'

I noticed that his wife was staring at me with an annoyed look on her face. I got up and sat beside her. I took one of her frail hands in mine and gently stroked her fingers. At once she relaxed and gave me a little smile.

'Tell me what you would like me to do, please?' I asked.

She reached into her cardigan pocket and gave me a list. I glanced through it.

'I'll try to do everything on here but if I can't I'll finish it up next time I come, in a couple of days, if that's all right with you?'

'Oh, yes please,' she said with a look of relief.

They had both been very disabled during their working lives but had worked full-time right up until their retirement. Now they were alone together day after day and I realised this was difficult for them. Both of them were argumentative and I hardly remember a day I went to them when they did not quarrel and break things in temper. Although she had been quiet the day I met her, I discovered that she was worse than her husband and was strong despite her disability. On one occasion she found a hammer and smashed their new gas cooker door with it. When I tried to remonstrate with her, she calmly said, 'Well, it's mine. I paid for it.'

'You will have to buy another one then, or use it as it is.'

I actually felt sorry for her poor husband, who could do little or nothing to stop her. That same afternoon she smashed the sink unit. Things were getting worse and I had no idea what to do. The problem was that she needed a lot of attention and seemed very jealous of her husband. He seemed a bit depressed with it all and without thinking I gave him a very brief hug. It was the wrong thing to do. His wife was so angry she shouted at me, calling me all the names she could think of while I stood there in bewilderment. I let her rant until she suddenly stopped and the tears ran down her cheeks. Her husband looked terrified.

'I should go into the bedroom for a minute,' I whispered and he wheeled himself quickly out of the room. I tried to comfort her as best as I could.

'Don't be so upset.'

'You like him better than me, I can tell!' she whimpered.

'Look,' I said, 'I go into many homes and to be honest, the only people I really love or care for are those in my own family. I don't prefer one client to another at all.'

This was brutal I know, but I felt I had to be honest to convince her I had no designs on her eighty-year-old husband. I took an envelope out of my bag and began showing her the photos of my family; my parents, husband

and four children as babies, all smiling and full of fun. She was entranced as she looked at each one.

'Can I have some of these?' she asked. I was puzzled at this request.

'Why would you want pictures of *my* family? Would you like to show me some of *your* family – your wedding photos perhaps?'

She hobbled over to a cupboard and brought out a box. She had very few photos to show me. She wore a jacket and skirt in her wedding photo and her mother stood beside them looking extremely miserable. I had an idea.

'I know what we could do! How would you like a professional photographer to come here and take a lovely photo of you both looking happy together?'

Her husband came out from his refuge and smiled.

'That sounds a lovely idea,' they both nodded. So it was arranged. It certainly gave them both something to look forward to. It turned out that they had both been brought up in a children's home and neither of them had seen much of their parents. They had endured an unhappy childhood but it was this common thread that drew them together and bound them in isolation.

As I gradually got to know them, I learned about the life that they had and what they had both been through. My heart went out to them. No wonder they were so unhappy. I would encourage them to be more positive whenever I could.

'You've got each other. You should go out more, even if it's just a walk to the shops. There are coach trips for the day or sit on a bench in the park on a sunny day. There are so many things you can do,' I suggested. 'I'll bring the paper in and we can see what's available.' Slowly but surely their lives improved as they tried to extricate themselves from the rut they had worn themselves into. Neighbours began to knock and ask if there was anything they needed and waved as they passed their window. The best thing of all was discovering that he used to play the accordion, he brought it out from its final resting place and began playing again. She rediscovered her artistic talents and began painting watercolours. It was a good start. Soon they had no time to spare. They did not change completely, but arguing, smashing up their home and being miserable were things of the past. They even began taking an interest in their small garden. She invited me to sit out there and have a cup of tea one summer day. We sat quietly and watched the bees and butterflies in the flowerbeds.

'Look, how pretty that butterfly is!' she commented.

'It is,' I replied. 'We used to see hundreds of them when I was a girl.'

For a moment I was lost in the memories of my own childhood, when the days were long and summer lasted until forever. I felt my hand being squeezed and, looking up, I saw my companion had tears in her eyes and a smile on her face.

'How lucky you were,' she sighed. I smiled in return. I knew that being able to appreciate that special moment was the greatest gift of all. Mr and Mrs Mackie died within six months of each other. I hope that their latter years were happier than their former.

'I have another client for you, Rosemary,' said Mrs Jordan, 'to replace Mr and Mrs Mackie.'

I jotted down the information on my rota sheet.

'Anything else?' I asked.

'Just that Mr and Mrs Mackie rang me once as they wanted me to know that you were very kind to them and that they didn't want anyone else as they were very well suited. Thought you would like to know.'

'Thank you,' I smiled. 'I'm glad.'

I loved the differences between the people I had been sent to help. I looked forward to meeting each one. I loved variety and I certainly met it in my daily life. No two clients were the same. I was sent to Rubbing Ruby just for the one day. That Monday morning, Mrs Jordan rang early to tell me to go to Ruby's home from nine until eleven.

I arrived at her house, which was small, set back and surrounded by trees, which made it very dank and dark. I would root out at least half of these, I thought to myself. I bet they keep the light out of the house. As I approached, I could hear a high-pitched voice singing, 'O what a friend we have in Jesus'. It stopped when I pushed the door and walked in. A rosy-cheeked lady, her steely grey hair braided into two plaits, met me. She gave me a short list of things that she needed me to do.

'When you've done that, you will have plenty of time to do the rubbing,' she said. Rubbing? What on earth does she mean by rubbing? Perhaps she wanted me to polish up her brass or silver. If so I was prepared to tell her that brass was not considered to be essential enough to spend time on and I was not supposed to do it. However, she might mean something else, so I left it at that for the time being.

'Do you always leave your doors open, Ruby?' I asked.

'Oh, yes,' she said airily, 'but I know everyone and they all know me around here.'

'Well you've never met me before. I could have been anyone.'

'Ah, but you're not are you? You look like a good girl. I was a Sunday school teacher for thirty years. I can always tell just by looking at someone.'

'Looks can be deceiving,' I warned. 'All your doors are wide open and you have some beautiful things. You must keep yourself safe. There are some very bad people about. You must lock your doors. Those trees make it very secluded. You would never know if you had an intruder.'

She smiled and shook her head. 'Never mind about that. Anyway, let's get on. I must keep at least half an hour for the rubbing.'

'I'm not supposed to clean brass or silver,' I explained. 'We must only do essential things that you cannot do for yourself.' She looked at me as though I had lost my senses.

'I know that, dear,' she smiled, patting my hand, 'but what could be more important than my rubbing?'

Just then the phone rang and she went to answer it. Puzzled, I started on the list. None of it was too difficult. I vacuumed and dusted and then changed her bed sheets, which I noticed were streaked with a pink greasy substance. They went into the machine on a cool wash, as instructed. I still had more than an hour left.

'Make us both a cup of tea, Rosemary,' she said, 'and have one of my home-made biscuits.'

I rarely ate anything when I was working as I would soon put on too much weight but her shortbread biscuits were gorgeous.

'The only thing I still bake these days,' she said, 'but they are very quick and easy to make. All made with butter.'

I could see the calories oozing out of them but it did not stop me having another. She was gratified to see me enjoying her baking.

'There!' she said, putting the dishes in the sink. 'We'll get on with the rubbing now.' She walked into the next room. 'I'll call you in about five minutes.'

While I was waiting, I wondered, what on earth does she want me to do?

'Come in and close the door!' she called out.

I walked into a pretty room with a bed in the centre. She was lying in the middle of it in her vest and knickers. On a low table next to the bed was a huge pot of what looked like red floor polish.

'Start with my neck and back and work down,' she directed. 'Make them good hard rubs!'

Now I knew what she meant by 'rubbing', I rubbed the 'polish' as I thought of it as firmly as possible into her poor old aching limbs, all the time fighting off the hysteria which threatened to burst out of me at any minute.

'My, you certainly know how to rub. You must have done it before!' she commended.

'No,' I said truthfully, 'I've never done it before.' In my head I thought, and I'll never do it again if I can help it. By the time I had finished 'the rubbing' I had left very little unrubbed and I ached all over. Even the backs of my legs hurt.

'Oh, thank you, dear. I feel *so* much better. You're very good at rubbing.'

'Yes, I think I may need rubbing myself one of these days. What's this mixture called?'

'It's just a recipe that my husband mixed up,' she said proudly, 'I've got quite a few pots left. I'll put some in a jar for you if you like.'

'No thanks. By the time I need it, it will probably have gone off.'

I tried to wash the stuff off my hands but they were stained for days and my back ached for even longer. I was not sent to Rubbing Ruby again, thankfully. When I asked my supervisor why I had not been told about 'the rubbing' she said she must have forgotten to tell me. I gave her the benefit of the doubt but I always asked if any 'rubbing' was involved after that when I was sent to anyone new. Quite a few of my old ladies believed in rubbing ointments and lotions into their skin. They always said it made them feel much better. I think it was the human touch they enjoyed; the contact of gentle hands and the thought that someone was prepared to give such a personal service to them. I have bathed many elderly ladies who were unable to do so themselves and I have often marvelled at how beautiful the skin on their bodies has remained despite the ageing process. Because it had not been exposed to the elements it was like a small child's skin.

My Granny used to go out in all winds and weathers collecting herbs of all kinds. She hung them from the ceiling of her hut until they were dry. The more they dried out, the stronger they smelled. During the winter, her hut gave off the aroma of potions, creams and lotions that she would concoct from these dried herbs. We would have them poured down our throats or rubbed on our chests to ward off various ailments and so we always reeked of whatever she had 'cured' us with. I do not know if Granny ever used any of these herself but the skin on her body was like a pearl. Once I saw her soaking her poor feet after a day out hawking with her heavy basket. Her skirts were up to her knees and her pretty legs looked like those of a teenager. Unfortunately she suffered from dreadful bunions. Every pair of shoes she bought was ruined because she had to cut holes in them to allow room for the lumps.

However, Granny was a very active woman; I never saw her just sit and do nothing. She always had a bowl of peas to shell or beans to cut. She never learned how to read but she knew how many pennies there were in a shilling and shillings in a pound. She had to. She could not afford to make mistakes. My mother helped her with her paperwork and her daughters – my aunts Amy, Betsy, Britt, Mary and Prissy – had all helped Granny in the running of her household. All the work would be finished by twelve o'clock so they would wash and change their clothes, soaking them in a bucket of cold water ready to be washed the next day. In summer they would sit on chairs outside in the sunshine or around Granny's range in the winter. They would reminisce about places they had been or people they had met, sometimes singing, arguing or laughing together. Even though they were in their late teens and early twenties they would often include us little ones, teaching us songs and laughing when we got the words wrong. Some of the songs would include a naughty word and we would, in all innocence, repeat them to our mothers.

'Who learned yer they words?' my father would ask, trying not to laugh.

'Can't me-member,' I replied. I knew something was a bit wrong so I never owned up to who had really taught me. It was a gadje boy at school who taught me a very rude rhyme. I had not realised this at the time. I loved songs and poetry and recited it in the teacher's hearing.

'Who taught you that poem, Rosemary?' she asked blandly. I thought I would put in a good word for my mother, who had taught me many things. 'Me mother, Miss,' I stated proudly.

Oh what calamity befell me after that! My poor mother, who never even used so much as a mild swear word, was so upset when the teacher challenged her with teaching me such an *unrepeatable* rhyme. When she denied it they looked so sternly at her, I knew I had done wrong.

'It wasn't me mam,' I blurted. I told them who it was and the boy was hauled in. He was more than pleased to own up, even beginning to recite it before being hastily shut up. Mum was so relieved.

'Why did you say it was me?'

'Well, you're so good at learning me mammy, I said it was you 'cos I wanted they teachers to know you're clever.'

'*Teaching*,' she corrected. 'Don't do it again, Rosie. Ask me first in future.' Something I always memembered ever after.

10

Honeysuckle

After Granny and Granfer died, Uncle Alfie was left on his own in Granny's place. He had never married but was always well taken care of by his sisters. He had regular hot meals and plenty of mugs of tea. He did not seem to be lonely. He often had visitors and whenever I went over to see Mum in her caravan I would always pop my head around the door of Granny's old hut and have a chat with him. He had taken in a Jack Russell whom he named 'Snowy'. He had been snow white as a puppy but unfortunately this was a handicap in a scrap yard because he was always rolling around in the dusty yard and then he would go to where the men were working and find a nice patch of oil to roll in. All the baths in the world could not keep Snowy clean.

One afternoon after work, my mother came to see me quite unexpectedly. I could tell by her face something grave had happened.

'It's bad news, Rosie. Uncle Alfie has died,' she said sadly.

I was so shocked. I had never seen Uncle Alfie ill, even with a cold, even though he worked outside in all weathers. Mum was very upset as she told me that she had just finished her dinner when she heard Snowy let out the most heart-rending howls, one after another.

'I knew that Alfie had died,' Mum said. 'The dog was letting us know.'

Granny's place, where Alfie had been living, remained empty for many years. I say 'empty' as no one lived there, but Aunt Betsy still polished the brasses and kept everything as it was when Granny and Granfer had lived. Aunt Betsy stayed on in her hut alone after Uncle Alfie died. Their girls, my cousins Violet and Lavinia, had grown up and also married so Aunt Betsy filled her days with cleaning her little hut and Granny's old place.

I remember Uncle Alfie with great affection. He and Freddy looked after my mother after Dad died, giving her Dad's 'share' of the scrap yard proceeds long after anything Dad had owned was sold. It had supplemented her small pension and my Aunt Betsy had always brought her over a huge hot meal every day for supper, so she had been well looked after as she grew older. That is the Romany way: to look after your own people, especially when they became too old to fend for themselves. So different to the people I went to who had no family or community to rely on.

Lou's little cottage stood in about half an acre of garden. Everything that could be crammed in it, was. All the colours of the rainbow were there and the perfumes assaulted the senses. I knew that she would be in her garden; all the elderly ladies I had met so far spent all their time in the open air. And why not? I thought. At least they stood a chance of meeting a passer-by. Often that was all the opportunity they had for a bit of conversation. That was why having a home help was so important to them. Yes, there she was, knee-deep in marigolds. Her lovely face broke into a wide smile and tears stood in her pretty brown eyes. I was soon to learn that Lou's eyes would fill up with tears or crinkle with laughter whether she was happy or sad; her emotions were very near the surface.

'Hello!' I greeted her.

'Ah yes,' said Lou, 'me new home help!'

She put her arms around me and kissed me on the cheek.

'I'm glad,' she said. 'I did see you coming up the road. You stopped and stroked that raggedy old ginger cat. Nobuddy ever pets that poor old man!'

Dear Lou. She had her faults but no one could ever dislike her. I grew to love her, faults and all. Her story was so sad, like many of my ladies who were born at the turn of the twentieth century. She was born to a farm labourer, a silent, cold man, and his wife, who had been in service as a lady's maid. Her mother had been taught to behave in company. She had been very attractive and her mistress had passed on her cast-off clothes to her so that she always looked beautiful.

'Me father hooked me mother like a fish,' said Lou, 'and she was wed before she knew it!'

Lou told me that her mother had borne eleven children but only six had lived.

'Me father said it was for the best but me mother never thought so. Me dear Mam never forgot any of them and still grieved over their little graves until she died. When I was nearly thirteen, me father said I should get me feet under somebody else's table and I had to leave home and me dear Mam ...' Lou broke off and wept. This was a story I was to hear many times but it never ceased to break my heart. But for now I needed to get on with my work. Lou took me around the back to a tumbledown lean-to. I assumed it was a shed but was shocked to learn that this was her kitchen. Next door to this was a room about six feet wide by ten or twelve long.

'This is me bedroom,' she said. I tried not to show my disbelief. It was nothing more than a hovel.

'Now come down this passage and turn right. That's me front room.'

Talk about whitened sepulchres. Outside was chocolate-box pretty and completely belied the interior of Lou's home. The smell of damp was overwhelming and the wallpaper was peeling off the walls.

'What's that?' I asked, pointing at the mould-blackened carpet.

'Oh, that's only toadstools.'

I could have picked a basket of them. Lou gave a cheeky giggle.

'I often wish they were mushrooms, I could cook a few for me breakfast!'

'Oh, Lou!' I gasped. I could no longer hide my disgust. She ignored my expression.

'I'm a lucky woman Rosie. I've got me cat and me dog. Well, he's next door's really but he visits me. I've got me lovely garden and this beautiful cottage.' I could not speak. I was choked.

'I'll show you upstairs, but be careful coming up!' she warned.

'Oh, I thought this was all there was!'

'Oh, no,' she said, opening a door which was hidden behind a curtain. The stairs were steep and uncarpeted. They were missing treads and the rest felt spongy as I put my weight on them.

'Be careful!' she warned me again. I did not need telling twice. As I neared the top I could feel a stiff breeze. Three doors were facing me. Lou opened one. I looked up. The ceiling had almost gone, along with part of the roof and I could see blue sky and clouds drifting past. All the furniture was rotting and the mattress on the double bed had been chewed by rodents. The smell of damp was oppressive. Sadly Lou stroked the bed head.

'This was mine and Tom's marriage bed,' she said softly. 'We had a very happy marriage.'

I looked carefully at the bed. I could see that it had been very beautiful once.

'It must have cost a lot of money,' I remarked.

'It was made by Tom's friend as a wedding gift. Tom died in that bed.'

'I'm so sorry,' I said, seeing the tears welling up in her eyes.

'He suffered terrible bad,' she sniffed, 'he had a condition which affected his lungs. It was caused by heliotrope gas.'

For a moment I thought I had misheard her. Heliotrope was just a colour to me. I did wonder if she made it up, but years later I did hear it mentioned on a TV programme. I gazed around at the horrendous mess.

'Lou,' I said as gently as possible, remembering what I had been told ('It's their home. Do nothing without their permission no matter how small.') 'This house is very dangerous for you to live in, you know. Have you ever thought of leaving it?'

At once I saw my mistake. Lou's eyes brimmed with tears and she grabbed my hands and almost fell to her knees.

'Oh no! No! Please don't tell! Don't tell, please! *Please!*' she cried, until I became quite scared that she was going to pass out. I knew I had done wrong.

'It's all right,' I soothed, 'I promise from the bottom of my heart that I will do nothing without your permission. I've seen your home and I can see you love it very much. I will do all I can to make you comfortable and safe.'

'I believe you Rosie. I trust you.'

'Come on Lou, I'll make you a nice cup of tea.'

I sat her at her kitchen table, which was covered in several layers of newspaper for a tablecloth. Seeing my look, she explained.

'I puts seven layers of newspapers on my table and I takes off one layer every day. Then I starts again.'

I thought her very ingenious and I told her so.

'I does the same with me pinny. I puts seven on of a Sunday, then every day I takes one off 'til I've used 'em up. Then I starts again!'

Why on earth does she not just put a clean one on every day? And did that mean she wore them to bed? But I had learned my lesson and I said nothing. Looking around the kitchen, I realised that she had no electric kettle and no gas or electric cooker.

'What do you cook on Lou?' She gazed at me in wonderment.

'Why, my little oil stove of course!'

She pointed to what I had previously passed without noticing. There, blazing in a corner with the kettle boiling away, adding more damp to the already streaming walls, was a little paraffin camping stove. Grabbing a cloth, I took the kettle off the stove and poured a little water into the teapot to warm it up. At once, a huge spider crawled out of the spout where it had been taking refuge. I decided that as it was not dead and I had not poured boiling water over its defenceless body, the teapot must be safe to use. In the following weeks, I was to discover that Lou's crockery, which she kept stacked on the table, was a refuge for any creepy crawlies around. So I started to rinse the cups out in hot water before I used them, saying that they were making our tea cold so I was warming them up. Dear Lou accepted this completely.

Lou told me more of her story. She had gone to work in the laundry of a children's home. She loved the little ones and tried to get work caring for them but the powers that be decided that she should work in the laundry. Lou had only been thirteen but had been expected to wash dirty nappies, sheets and all manner of dirty linen by hand. One older woman would help her lift the clothes out of the boiler. She was wasting away with all the heavy work and the food that she and the other young workers were given was not enough to keep them going. She often had to pass through the kitchen when cakes and biscuits were being made but was never offered one even once as everything was counted. I had heard of this sort of thing many times before and was not surprised that Lou craved sweet food and ate too much of it.

Meanwhile, I was trying to sort out the mystery of her missing cooker. Lou told me that the cooker she once had was old but worked very well. Then two men came and told her they were taking it away because it was too old to be converted and so it was condemned.

'How long ago was this, Lou?'

'Oh it was months ago! I do miss being able to cook my Sunday dinner.'

'Did these men give you any forms or letters?'

'Yes,' she said, rummaging through her cutlery drawer, 'it's here somewhere.' She gave me a large brown envelope. 'Is this it?'

I checked through the paperwork. I saw that Lou had been without a cooker for more than five months. It had been deemed too dangerous and had been removed at once.

'I told the men I couldn't afford a new cooker,' said Lou, tears raining down her face.

'What did they say to that, then?'

'They said, "Social will sort it missus." I said, "I've got no money." Then they left and gave me that envelope.'

I was angry. How cruel to leave her in this state, I thought. Suddenly Lou began to giggle.

'Oh, Rosie, you do look so cross!' she laughed. I was not laughing.

I took the envelope into the gas company at the first opportunity and told the girl at the desk what had happened. Neither she nor her manager could explain why Lou had not had her cooker replaced. When I told him that this elderly lady had been cooking for five months on a dangerous camping stove they were very apologetic.

'We'll send her a bouquet of flowers and a new cooker with our compliments,' he grinned. I thought of Lou's flower-filled garden.

'That would be wonderful, but the flowers would be like sending coals to Newcastle! Why not send her a nice piece of beef? She hasn't had a roast dinner for months!' I suggested. Then, seeing a stack of stainless-steel saucepans on the counter, I added, 'And a set of saucepans wouldn't go amiss. She's ruined all hers by cooking on that little camping stove.'

He screwed up his eyes as if contemplating this latter suggestion.

'As a gesture of goodwill?' I said. 'I wouldn't like to think what would have happened if this lady had had a serious accident and having to explain that to the Gas Board.' He looked at me sideways.

'You drive a hard bargain, young lady,' he relented.

Well, I'm not my father's daughter for nothing, I thought. A few days later, Lou was waiting for me at her gate. She looked excited.

'Oh, come and see, Rosie!' she gushed. Her new cooker had been installed and stood gleaming in the gloomy kitchen. There, in pride of place on the table, was her new set of shiny saucepans and a new kettle. Opening the door of her fridge, I saw a nice joint of beef.

'They say I don't have to pay for anything! I can't believe it!' she smiled.

Lou never used her saucepan set. She just kept them on the table displayed for all to see. She used her cooker often and kept it spotless, wiping it and polishing it constantly, even when it did not need it.

I stayed with Lou for several years. She was a kind woman but she did have an unfortunate habit of giving things away to people she hardly knew, regretting it almost at once and expecting me to ask them for it back. I found this very humiliating. It was something I would never do myself. Lou would suddenly decide that she could not live without the article and decided that Tom had given it to her and she must have it back *now*. She would stand there in floods of tears, asking me to get it returned to her.

'No Lou,' I said firmly, 'it's not the right thing to do. How would you feel if someone gave you a gift and then asked you to return it?' I felt like I was reasoning with a child.

'Please,' she begged, 'Tom bought it for me. I've just remembered.'

'Sorry, no.'

In the end, I waited until the friend popped in when I was there and in front of Lou I told her that Lou wanted the gift returned. Lou did not look at all bothered. Her friend looked uncomfortable to say the least.

'It would be better if you told your friends not to accept anything from you in future Lou, in case you forget and want it back,' I said, looking her straight in the eye. 'My mother would have been very cross with me if I did such a thing as it is very bad-mannered, and also cruel. In the future, if you want something returned you must do it yourself.'

'I'm sorry, Rosie. I won't do it again,' she apologised. She *did* ask me to do it again but I always refused. I could never understand how adults could do this yet I came across it many times.

The time I spent with Lou opened my eyes wider to things I had already noticed. Many of the things most gadjes did were no different to the way Gypsies did them and yet there were some things that were definitely done differently. Gypsy Granny in particular would never have used a multi-purpose bowl. She had an aluminium bowl for each purpose: one for the dishes, one for the veggies, one for baking purposes, another for the dishcloths – all kept separate and scoured until they gleamed like silver. So were her saucepans and frying pans. Her tea towels and dishcloths were boiled each day until they were snowy white. When I first went into people's homes as a home help, I was shocked to see the disgusting state of some of their dishcloths. They looked and smelt vile and some of the tea towels could have stood up on their own. Although Lou was very poor, she had spotlessly clean towels and cloths. One elderly man who I went to only had one tea towel. I went there once a week and by the time I returned, his tea towel was black. I would encourage him to buy a few more but old habits die hard. I took my own little bottle of bleach so I could at least leave his tea towel clean. This was the seventies and hygiene in the kitchen did not have the advantage of anti-bacterial cleansers then.

Long after Lou had gone into a nursing home and passed away, I would point out her cottage to my children as we passed on our way to the beach. The garden still overflowed with flowers and honeysuckle crawled over the porch roof, just as Lou would have wanted it to.

11

Daisy of the Veldt

Most of my clients were from humbler backgrounds, but one in particular was in a class of her own. I named her 'the African Queen' after only one day. I had walked to her house the first morning. From the moment I opened the gate I was in Fairyland. The small garden was stuffed with more flowers and plants than I had ever seen in such a small space. The buzzing of bees filled the air and butterflies fluttered around the buddleia tree. I was in heaven. As I approached the front door I saw several tiny mice lined up in a neat row on the step and all very dead. The door was ajar, so I stepped over them and knocked loudly.

'Is anyone in?' I called.

'Yes,' a quavery voice called back. 'Come in, do!'

To my immediate right there was another door, slightly open. I walked into a gloomy and what I thought was an empty room. The curtains were drawn shut and in a chink of sunlight I could see a wrinkled old hand, complete with a cigarette in a long holder, resting on the arm of a chair. In it sat a very tiny, wrinkled old lady. That was my first sight of the African Queen. She smiled at me, showing a set of pearly white false teeth. As usual, I introduced myself and explained that Social Services were allowing her two hours three times a week. She grumbled at this, saying she needed someone there every day.

'I don't mind paying. I can afford it!' she insisted. That was not the issue.

'I need you to sort my clothes out and get my lunch,' she went on.

'What do you mean, sort your clothes out?'

She pointed to a door on the other side of the room. I went over and tried to push the door open but there was something behind it. I gave it a great heave and to my dismay I saw that she had taken every item of clothing out of two huge old wardrobes and piled them on the bed, chair and floor. The smell of mothballs was overpowering.

'Why have you done this?' I asked.

'I was looking for a decent garment to wear.'

'Why, are you going somewhere important?'

'No. Does it matter?'

'Yes,' I said firmly, 'I'm not here to pick up after your forays in the wardrobe. You will have to pick up after yourself.'

She looked shocked. I reasoned that if she was able to unhook every item off the hangers, she was able to hang them back on.

'My other home help used to do it,' she said. More fool her, I thought.

'You emptied it out. I'm afraid you will have to put it back. I'll start your lunch.'

She stood up looking helpless. Then she spoke the words I was to hear over and over during the next couple of years.

'When I was in Africa, the maids did *everything*.'

'Well, you're in England now and I'm not a maid.'

'Can you cook?' she asked.

'My family never complains.'

'Well, there's some chicken in the fridge. Make me my favourite dish. My African cook made it for me often. Lemon chicken and boiled rice.'

This was more than forty years ago when the only TV chefs we had were Fanny Cradock or Tony Stoppani on our regional programme. I was a good plain cook like my Granny in Town but I had cooked nothing more exotic than Lancashire hotpot. I had been directed by my boss to cook plain, healthy but simple meals.

'I'll see what I can do,' I conceded. I stir-fried her chicken in a pan with butter and lemon juice while I boiled some plain rice and then made a sauce with the lemon juice and butter I had cooked. I found some parsley in the garden and pinched the tip off and added it to the dish as a garnish. I had just done my best but I thought it looked quite good. I hoped she thought so too when I placed it in front of her. She looked at it but made no comment.

'Get me a large sherry,' she demanded. I poured her out a large schooner and offered it to her.

'No, no. Not *that* glass. The large one.' She pointed to a huge goblet that must have held almost half a bottle of sherry and asked me to top it up. She took a sip and then started on the lemon chicken. She ate and drank the lot.

'That was very nice my dear,' she said to my surprise. She fell asleep while I washed up. I was quietly pleased initially. The trouble was, every time I visited her after that, she had some exotic menu that she wanted me to cook. I asked her what was in it and then used the basic ingredients to knock up a few interesting meals. I soon got the reputation of being 'a wonderful cook'. That made me laugh, but I think being able to cook is in my blood. I think of Granny in Town and my mother cooking on a tiny range with no thermostat. Mum did have a disaster one day. She put a joint in the oven surrounded by potatoes and went out to the garden. Meanwhile, Dad put more coal on the fire, forgetting to tell my mother. When Mum came in, smoke was everywhere and the food was charred to a cinder. Dad owned up but at least Mum was not to blame. We ended up with toast. It was just another day but toast doesn't taste as good as roast beef and taters.

At the end of three weeks, the African Queen was still putting away her clothes. Every time she asked me to do it, I refused. I knew that if I agreed she would try this little trick with something else.

'If you put it all away yourself you will know where everything is and you will never have to take everything out again,' I reasoned with her.

'Ohh,' she moaned. Here it comes again, I thought, 'When I lived in Africa, my maid did all this for me!'

'Poor girl,' I said. She looked at me in outrage.

'I was very kind to my servants. They ate as well as we did!'

'I'm pleased to hear it. But this is England. We have no servants here,' I reminded her. 'If you make too much work for me, I will never get you sorted out. You must look after your own clothes.'

The African Queen had lived in Africa all her married life. Her husband had been a scientist. She had been spoilt and indulged all her life and she had one child, a son who I had never seen. She said she saw him once a year. She had sent him to England when he was just five years old to be educated at an exclusive boarding school. Now his parents were strangers to him. She often complained that he rarely came to see her ever since she had returned to England in her late forties. She had grandchildren that she had never seen. How sad, I thought. I think of my weekends at home now, which are full of children and grandchildren, raucous laughter and chatter until I shut the door behind them. She may have thought that she had had a wonderful life in Africa but now the only thing that she gained affection from was her enormous black cat: the bringer of dead mice and other sundry dead animal gifts. All over the kitchen and other downstairs rooms were dishes of rotting cat food. I threw it, dishes and all, into the dustbin and told her it was very bad for her health having all this rotting maggoty food in the house. I showed her the maggots and told her she had a rat in the garden. I had to get the pest control officer in to fumigate. She actually seemed glad for me to take over and soon she was mice- and rat-free. Her cat was her precious friend but even he was full of worms and fleas and had to go to the vet. 'Tiddles' was the ugliest cat I had ever seen. His ears were torn and his tail looked as though it had been eaten off. His molars grew over his bottom lip and he smelled but the African Queen loved him. I explained that as he was an outdoor cat and ate rats, mice and other garbage, it was dangerous for her to let him lick her face. She was a bit upset by this but she did stop him. Life at her house was a lot better after this for everyone. It was good not to have to worry about treading in cat food or other unmentionables.

The African Queen had always had a washerwoman to do her laundry. Even her most delicate and lacy undies were washed and ironed to perfection.

'Don't expect me to iron your knickers,' I said. 'I don't even iron my own.'

'Why doesn't that surprise me,' she said wryly.

'I haven't been as lucky as you were. Washing for four children and two adults, going out to work every day, coming back and cleaning a four-bedroom house and then cooking a hot dinner for six every night, *plus* doing a huge shop twice a week doesn't leave me much time for ironing knickers!' I said breathlessly. She suddenly burst out laughing.

'No, I don't suppose it does!'

After that, she did not ask me to do much that she could not do herself. She did ask me to wash one of her best dresses. It looked expensive; a crêpe de chine that should never be washed.

'I think this needs to be dry cleaned,' I said, examining the washing instructions.

'Just give it a cool wash,' she said. I refused.

'It will be ruined.' I often took her heavier wash home and put it through my own machine. 'Please, have your dress dry cleaned. It will only cost a few pounds,' I said as I was going home on Friday.

Monday came around all too soon. It was a warm sunny day and the African Queen was in her front garden cutting a few flowers. She loved her garden and we had a lot in common with our love for nature. It was a joy just to walk around her flowerbeds and she would tell me about the exotic flowers she had grown in her African garden.

'I'll just hang my coat up,' I called back as I stepped through her open front door. I walked straight through to the kitchen when something caught my eye outside the window. What *was* that on the washing line? I thought. I stepped outside and saw what remained of the African Queen's posh dress. It was horrific. The lining had not shrunk at all, but the gorgeous crêpe de chine had shrivelled so badly, the dress would have fitted a five-year-old. The lining hung down inches longer than the dress. I turned as I heard her footsteps behind me. She could not meet my horrified gaze.

'Can you stretch it, do you think?' she asked in a small voice.

'No,' I said, reaching up and unpegging it. She placed it in the bin and was very quiet for the rest of the day. It did not cure her. She still thought she was always right.

She asked me to buy a gift for her son on her behalf. I expected her to tell me exactly what she wanted, where to buy it and the price she was willing to pay. I also asked her to ring my office and tell them that she was giving me a large sum of money with which to buy it.

'Oh what a muddle! I trust you. Isn't that enough?' she whimpered.

'Yes, you can trust me but unfortunately, I can't be sure that you might just forget how much you gave me. It happens sometimes. I just need you to contact the office.'

After this was sorted, I went into town as she had asked; I bought the gift and delivered it safely into her hands. I called in a neighbour to witness it for me. She thought this very strange and funny but with elderly forgetful people we had to protect ourselves. It was better to be safe than sorry. Her son sent her a plain 'Thank you' card and nothing else. The African Queen was in tears afterwards.

'My own flesh and blood! We gave him the best that money could buy: education, holidays, good clothes and he thinks more of *strangers* than he does of me!'

I felt deeply sorry for her. She could not see that this man's parents had been strangers to *him*. Money, clothes and holidays meant nothing when all he had needed was a loving family. I immediately thought of the little I had in a material way as a child: a basic education, basic food and *never* a holiday. But I did have a loving family community, good homegrown food and long happy days spent in the Somerset countryside. I had my parents and my brothers and cousins around me, a song and a campfire and I was tucked up each night in my little wooden bed in the wagon we called 'home'.

She never went anywhere. I tried to encourage her.

'Why don't you book a coach trip, or go out for lunch?' I suggested. 'You said you used to enjoy whist drives.'

'What?' she exclaimed, 'Go out with a lot of old ladies?'

She drew deeply on her cigarette. I knew what was coming next.

'When I was in Africa, I was invited *everywhere*. I was the belle of all the balls. My clothes and jewellery were admired by everyone. We had a *wonderful* life.' She looked dreamily out of the window.

'Why did you come back to England then?' I asked.

'My husband, whom I adored, died. I was left alone. I didn't even know how to write a cheque. I had to come back. If I didn't live in this little cottage rent-free I would probably be in the workhouse.'

'There are no workhouses now,' I said, 'and this is a lovely little cottage.'

'The roof leaks.'

I knew that but I had not realised that her little cottage was a grace and favour home and was held in trust through the family. It did not belong to her. That hardly mattered, though – until some months later that is.

I arrived as usual one morning to find men on the roof and a large roll of lead in the garden. They seemed to be replacing this with cheap tar paper. I called up to them.

'What are you doing? And why have you removed the lead from the roof?' I demanded. They glanced quickly at each other.

'What do you mean, "lead?"' said the older one. The other man continued working.

'Get down immediately and come and speak to me or I'm ringing the office.'

'How do *you* know what we're doin'? And what business is it o' yourn?'

I went straight in and asked the African Queen what the men were doing on the roof.

'They're fixing the leak,' she told me, blankly. I rang the office immediately and they rang the police who arrived shortly after. The men had disappeared.

'Leave the lead where it is. It's too heavy to move,' said the young policeman. The next day, I arrived at the cottage to find that the lead had been removed but not by the police. Hundreds of pounds' worth, gone. The African Queen paid to have the tiles replaced and tar paper was used instead of the lead. This let the rainwater in like a waterfall and ruined some of her nice things. How did I know that it was lead that had been stripped from the roof? I knew at a glance. I had not been brought up by a man who dealt in scrap metal and learned nothing. My father and uncles had made a living with scrap metal and I was used to seeing the lead weighed out on the large old weighing scales and then melted down into a lump. My father was a Romany and probably sailed a bit close to the wind sometimes but I know he would never have done anything to harm a defenceless person. We were all brought up to be honest on our camp. We had to be more honest than any gadje, Dad said, because 'yer would be the first to 'ave the finger pointed at yer!' I always remembered what he told me and it has always stood me in good stead.

The African Queen eventually went into a residential

home. She had only been there a week when she began to go missing. Several times a week she would make her way back to her cottage in the village and would sit quietly in her garden until a kind neighbour would gently take her back. She only lived a short time after that. I did not go to her funeral but I sent a small bouquet, which I picked from her beloved garden, and a small card, which read:

'I'll miss you, dear African Queen, Rosemary.'

12

Thrift

All the time I worked for Social Services, I was caring for men, women, old and young. Many through age or disability were unable to cope with everything themselves when they were alone with no family around to help. Most lived in and around the same small village near the seaside until well in to their eighties or nineties. I noticed that whether they were poor or well off, they all took great care of their money; not in a mean way, but never wasting any. They were careful with their tea bags, bread and other basics. I often had a cup of tea which tasted flat and looked grey with no body to it. I thought perhaps it was the cheapest brand bought for the help to use, but no, they would drink the same. They would usually offer me a biscuit or a small cake with it, so it was not meanness; therefore I was surprised one morning when I saw eight or nine tea bags hanging on a little line in the sunshine in Mrs Kenn's kitchen window. I did not mention it to her then but after she asked me to wipe out her fridge, I found a bag of bits of bread, more than a little green in parts.

'Is this for the birds?' I asked.

'No, of course not. I can make a nice little pudding out of that.'

'It isn't very healthy. You can get ill eating stuff like this.'

'It's very clear that you've never gone without,' she remarked bitterly. 'My dear husband died shortly after returning from Burma. He was skin and bone and he died because he was starved nearly to death in the camp where he was incarcerated. When he returned home he couldn't eat or even digest the food we bought specially for him. He wanted to and he tried very hard but it was too late and he died very young. I miss him still.'

'That's very sad,' I said.

'I was lucky enough to have this little house. I was born here. After my husband died, I went home to take care of my dear parents, but nothing will take the place of my dear husband.' She picked up a photograph off a cabinet. 'Isn't he handsome in his uniform?'

'Yes, he is indeed,' I agreed, as I looked at the young face. She smiled.

'We met when we were at nursery school. We lived just a few doors away from each other. Very few days passed when we didn't see each other.'

She dusted his photo with her hanky and replaced it on the cabinet with a little sigh.

'He's been dead for more than forty years now,' she said, 'and I've missed him ever since. Every afternoon, I go to bed early. The days pass more quickly then.'

I could not believe how lonely she was. One day, I happened to mention how my husband John and our children all loved wildlife.

'At the moment, we have two very large hedgehogs in our garden. We love to watch them feed. We have all sorts of different birds which visit, all the year round, and we have a wood mouse under our shed.'

'Oh,' she said, 'I wish I could watch the birds and animals!'

'Look at your huge garden!' I said, 'you'll have all sorts in there. It just needs thinning out a bit so you can see.'

We got her garden sorted with hanging bird feeders and animal feeders to encourage the hedgehogs. Soon after, a fox visited, which thrilled her to bits. Soon I was enjoying her birds; so many kinds.

'Listen to the blackbird,' she would say. 'What a joyous song!'

Another time she could not wait to announce that she had recognised a song thrush.

'I'm beginning to know the songs and the names of all of them. There's even a starling who sounds like a "Trim" phone,' she enthused. The most exciting moment of all was when a robin built its nest in the ivy and when two little baby robins made an appearance one warm day; she was so happy. She sat in her window all day long with the special field glasses she had bought for the purpose. She had bought videos and books, spending some of the money she had saved. She then bought as many plants as she could which would attract bees and insects, including a beautiful buddleia, which would entice the butterflies. Then she had a pond put in to attract some gorgeous dragonflies. She even went so far as to plant a special nettle, which to my amazement lured many butterflies and winged insects. Her tatty old garden had become a wild bird and insect sanctuary.

'To think,' she sighed one day, 'I was just getting through each day. Look what I would have missed!'

'Well you must have deeply loved all these wonderful things. You just needed someone to show you what was there all the time.'

'You must have had a wonderful teacher,' she said to me. 'Who was it that showed you how to recognise these things?'

Do you know, I had to think about it, because there never was just one.

'I was brought up in a very large family. There was always someone to show me or answer my question. I had wonderful grandparents. My own father took the time to show my brothers and me so many interesting things – even a family of otters once. That was an unforgettable day: a picture in my memory that never leaves me.'

My Granfer would take us to collect the horse and we would dawdle all the way home, asking questions and having them answered in a sensible way. Mrs Kenn had a tear in her own eye as I described Johnny and all the amazing stories that he told, never really expecting you to believe him.

'Oh, my dear girl,' said Mrs Kenn, 'you must have been very rich to own horses and to spend so much time having holidays in the countryside! We also lived here by the seaside and country but my mother and father both worked very hard to buy this house. They paid three hundred pounds for it; a lot of money then and my mother worked in a tea shop!'

Granny's 'bit o' ground' had cost her one hundred and fifty pounds back in the late 1930s. This lady had a house in a seaside village that had not cost a lot more and yet eight to ten families had lived on Granny's ground when I was a child. I replied that no, we had not been rich in a monetary way at all. Granfer had trained horses in wartime but then he had given up working for the government as he found it difficult to surrender his horses for cannon fodder. He had plenty of other things to do without that. Granfer had a few horses. They were little more than pets, Billy Pony being our favourite.

Mrs Kenn asked me a few more questions but I was being wary. I did not want to tell her too much about my life. She was not a gossip but I thought it better to be discreet. She sat down by the open window and began peeling an orange.

'My,' she said, 'this orange is so juicy! Can you get me a damp cloth?'

When I returned with the cloth a few moments later, my heart turned over. She was so still that for a moment I thought she had passed away. Then I noticed that the dish of orange segments was covered in quivering butter-flies, all feeding. She was gazing at the scene, entranced. I crept softly towards her and we sat in silence for several minutes until they fluttered gently away. We stared at each other in amazement.

'What a thrilling sight!' she gasped. 'If I never see another butterfly, I will remember this!'

I smiled as I recalled my own special memory of a field full of butterflies. The time in my childhood when one warm summer day, two little Gypsy girls peeped over a gate into a field and saw what they thought was a field full of beautiful blue flowers. Suddenly, like a breath of air, a cloud of butterflies flew up as one, softer than a sigh. Then they were gone, all except one, which had settled on one of my long plaits. This memory has stayed with me all my life.

'Yes,' I said, 'I saw a wondrous sight such as this many years ago as a child.'

Mrs Kenn smiled at me. 'How wonderful!'

'All my life it has been like a beautiful jewel that I could take out and gaze at if I ever felt I needed to.'

'And now I have a special memory, too,' she said. 'My very own.'

Yes, she had certainly come out of her shell. She was a different woman; a happier woman with so much to look forward to.

Some of her bad habits were still there. Miracles, I had been told, would take a little longer.

'Have you seen my hairbrush?' she asked me one morning.

'What hairbrush? You mean that old one you hang up by the hall mirror?'

'Ha!' she said. 'You *have* seen it!'

'I wondered why you were hanging on to it. It's no good is it?'

'I've had that hairbrush since I was fourteen,' she looked at me accusingly, 'and now it's *gone*!'

I felt very annoyed with her. I had done so much to

help her. Yes, I knew that it was my job and I got paid for it but to be accused of taking her hairless hairbrush was just ridiculous. She could see I was cross.

'Do you know,' I said, 'I am a home help to a very nice old gentleman of nearly a hundred years old. He was a gardener. One day he asked me where his tin opener had gone. He had had it when he was in the trenches, fifty-five years before. "Well, it's about time you had another then," I said. No, no he wanted *that* one. I looked *everywhere* for it. Finally I said, "Do you think I've taken your tin opener?" "No, my dear, why would you do that?" he said. "Exactly," I said, "I've got two or three spare ones at home, I'll bring you in one." "I want my old one," he said. I said no more but on the way out, I checked the bin. No, it wasn't in there. He'd gone out to his shed and put on his overall coat. He called me back. His tin opener was in his hand. Looking very guilty he said, "I remember now, going out the back way. I put my opener in my pocket and then I took my coat off and forgot it was there." "That's all right then," I said and went home. The next time I went he presented me with a big bouquet of flowers from his greenhouse.'

Mrs Kenn said nothing and I forgot about it.

The next time I went to see her I gave the bathroom a good clean and found the errant brush in the laundry basket. It was just a simple wooden-handled one with no more than a few bristles left.

'If I were you, I would give it a good wash and then put it away. It's no good as a brush any more and of no value to anyone except to you. No one else would want it, would they?'

'I'm sorry,' she said. 'I know it's of no value but I remember being given it as a young girl and I'd just hate to lose it.'

When I went into town to meet Mum at the weekend, Woolworths had some similar-shaped hairbrushes on sale so I bought one for Mrs Kenn.

'Oh, you shouldn't have!' she said.

'Just don't lose it,' I joked. She never used it but kept it in pride of place on her little dressing table. It is no good belittling anyone's funny ways. We all have them. We keep little worthless keepsakes that mean nothing at all to others but mean so much to us.

My dear and much-loved Granfer had a little silver pocket comb. He had owned it for so long it had worn thin where his fingers had rubbed it in the same place. He would sit in front of the range, his feet on the fender, combing his silvery hair into a kiss curl and Granny would hand him his mug of tea.

'Sit down yer Mary Ann, you'm allus on the go. 'Ave yerself a cuppa tea.'

Granny and Granfer would have what the gentry called 'afternoon tea', sharing Granfer's bit of toasted bread. What a picture they made. I have no need of a photograph. It is all in my head; two old people sitting in the dusk in front of a glowing range, eating toast and drinking hot tea.

Granny had given Granfer the little comb many years before. It was hallmarked silver. A posh lady had asked Granny to read her palm. Granny had agreed. When the lady opened her purse to pay Granny with a silver coin, Granny spotted the comb.

'My lady!' says Granny, playing up to her a bit, 'Instead of half a crown, could 'ee give I that little comb? I would love it so fer me own dear husband!'

The lady said yes at once, thinking she had a bargain. She laid the comb in Granny's hand and Granny told her everything that she wanted to know. At the end of the telling, both were well and truly satisfied. Granny gave Granfer the little silver comb that afternoon. It was his most treasured possession.

The silver comb was real silver and Granfer loved it.

'I've never sin another like it,' he would say, rubbing it up with his handkerchief. One day, he thought he had lost it. Everything was turned upside down in the quest to find it. Granny too was upset because Granfer was. In the end she gave up but Granfer would not.

'I can't rest until I finds it,' he said, going through the pockets of an old coat once more.

'I'll get another fer 'ee my Edwin. Don't worry over it.'

'Mary Ann, it won't be the same will it?' he said mournfully. Granny took the coat from him and, turning it inside out, she ran her fingers down the seams.

'Well!' she shouted. 'What's this then?' and, pushing her fingers through a hole in the lining, she pulled out the little silver comb! Granfer's face was a picture. He smiled from ear to ear and all day long he took it out of his pocket, gave it a rub and then replaced it. Shaking his head from side to side, he kept repeating: 'I can't believe it! I just can't believe it!'

On the day that he was buried, Granny combed his

kiss curl for the last time, tucked the comb into his jacket pocket and kissed his forehead.

'Goodnight my Edwin,' she whispered. She stood with her head bent for a little while but she was never again to hear him say, 'Goodnight my Mary Ann.'

My own mother had kept a little box of worthless things that meant everything to her. I, too, have little things that the children have given me: a little wooden mouse with blue pins for eyes and a tiny piece of leather for a tail from Daniel, and from Claire a pretty little stool. From my daughter Virginia I have a beautiful ornament, a figurine of a young girl made of onyx and marble; the golden-coloured stone depicts long blonde hair on the head and the marble-like material her dress. It reminds me of her every day. On a holiday she had in Cornwall, she spent every penny of her pocket money on this lovely thing. Virginia was not clever with her hands like the other children but her generosity was boundless and I have many things she gave me over the years. Sarah, my eldest, has also given me many things. I have stopped them from buying me anything else for the house, as I am getting crowded. Although, I am very proud of a beautiful pink and silver box made of a delicate, transparent, shell-like material with silver filigree threads and butterflies, which Sarah and her husband Alan gave me when my first book, *A Field Full of Butterflies*, was published. I would hate to lose any of these keepsakes, even if they appear worthless to others.

One of my clients had gone to live with her daughter. I was happy for her. She had been getting a bit forgetful so it was the best thing for her. Now I was going to someone new. She lived in a Victorian house facing the sea. She opened the door almost as soon as I knocked. She was tall and thin with a wide smile. As many of my new clients did, she invited me to have a cup of tea and I introduced myself.

'Can I call you Rose?' she asked, 'and you can call me Maude.'

As we approached the kitchen door a high-pitched scream made me jump. Then I realised that she was singing in a high soprano voice. Then she rattled the door handle loudly before entering. She quickly glanced around the kitchen and, instinctively, so did I.

'Sit down, dear, and I'll make us a nice cuppa.'

I sat down. She took the teapot to the cooker and poured boiling water into the pot. Then she brought the pot and teacups to the table. The tea was pale grey, thin and tasteless. It was not the first or last cup of tea I was offered made with used teabags. It was horrid and I did not drink it. I noticed a huge pile of heavy washing on the floor.

'I'll take that home for you if you like and put it through my machine. It won't take long.'

'Oh, I'll pay you,' she said.

'No, I'm not allowed to take money,' I told her. 'That's a very strict rule. I'm paid already by the council.'

Sometimes, I liked to do a few extras for 'my ladies'. These were my 'love jobs', done for free, as I like to think that not everything should have a price tag. Besides, they had to take care of the money they did have. Maude had a thing about electricity, though, always switching things off when I least expected it. Like when I was carrying the vacuum downstairs one day. I screamed out in shock when everything suddenly went dark.

'What's the matter? Are you all right?' she shouted up.

'I nearly fell!'

'I didn't know where you were.'

'I could have broken my leg. Then what would you say?'

'I'd say you fell and broke your leg,' she said dryly.

She switched the light back on and I put the vacuum under the stairs. I went to go into the kitchen but she barged past me, making loud humming noises and quickly looking around. What was she doing?

'If you could take home my curtains and covers, you can wash the lighter things in there,' she said, pointing to a wreck in the corner.

'You'll have to show me how it works, or else give me the instruction book.'

'What do you call yourself?' she asked sarcastically. 'Not able to use a washing machine?'

She looked at me sideways.

'What are you finding so funny?'

'I'm just thinking of my father. He brought home a washing machine for my mother. It was a kind thought but when my mother tried to use it, her washing looked dirtier when she finished than when she started! She only used it once. It was sent for scrap.'

'Was your father in the business of scrap dealing then?' she asked.

'Yes, among other things.'

'Oh, where did you live?'

'In the country,' I replied, 'but I'm here to help you so we had better get on.' I could see she wanted to know more but I did not want to tell her my business.

'What was that?' I said, peering under the table.

'What was what?' she asked, looking everywhere but under the table.

'Yes! There's a mouse!' I pointed.

'Oh, I don't think so dear,' she said casually, walking towards the living room door. She opened it and then I saw them. Mice. Everywhere. I froze and then let out a scream. She came back looking like butter wouldn't melt.

'What is it my dear? It's only a mouse or two. They won't hurt you.'

I realised that was why she was singing and making a noise. She was trying to get rid of the mice before I saw them. It also explained why there were lots of little black bits on the living room carpet when I vacuumed it.

'They don't do any harm,' she reasoned. 'They keep my floor clean, eating all the crumbs.'

'Yes,' I said, fighting my desire to stand on a chair, 'and they leave their droppings everywhere, they're filthy and they cause diseases. You could become very ill.'

'I'm well into my nineties so that doesn't worry me.'

'Well, it worries me,' I said. They were even climbing up the tatty wallpaper and eating the paste. I thought that had fungicide in it.

'The paste is made from flour and water. We couldn't get the stuff you buy today,' she explained, 'so we had to mix up our own.'

'How long has this paper been on the wall?'

'Now,' she said, counting on her fingers, 'let me see. Thirty or forty years I'd say.'

That did not surprise me a bit. It was hanging off in strips and there was no colour or pattern left in it.

'Maude, I think I'm going to have to speak to someone in my office. I think your home will have to be fumigated. The mice will have to go.'

She looked disappointed.

'If you want pets I suggest a couple of cats, preferably neutered unless you want to exchange mice for kittens. It would be a good idea to get the garden looked over as well. I'm sure I saw a rat down by the bins earlier.'

I was not sure of this, as I had not hung around long enough to find out. It took weeks to rid the house of vermin. In the end three houses in the row had to be rid of mice and rats. I got the blame for this. It seems that getting rid of the vermin at Maude's had sent them running into the neighbours' properties. While I worked in that small village, I saw more mice than I had ever seen in my life. Most of the homes I visited had a mouse if not several dozen in residence but the homes were very old and it seemed a natural habitat for them. Maude baulked at throwing away packets of food that had been chewed by the mice. They probably all returned after a few years. One of Maude's neighbours made me laugh.

'I'm a bag of nerves,' she said.

'Why?'

'It's so quiet now, I can't relax, I keep waiting for the clang of the mouse traps!'

I smiled, thinking that she was joking, but she was serious. In fact, I knew what she meant. I used to set traps for a very elderly man, but I always hoped I would not hear the 'snap' of the mousetraps because I would never empty them. I would just bring them in on a shovel covered with kitchen paper and the dear wheel-chaired gentleman would dispose of them. Fortunately he did not mind.

Once the work had been done to renovate her home, she relaxed completely. Her house looked very nice. I was still her home help but because she was so elderly I accompanied her on her visits to the bank, post office and shopping trips. The bus was always full and Maude had a field day, chatting to all and sundry. That would have been fine, except she chattered about where she went, what days she went and what time she came back. She boasted about her bright new home. She even informed everyone that I was her 'helper' and proceeded to tell them the days and times I came. I tried hard to stop her. I gave her little pep talks.

'Please, *please*,' I begged her, 'don't talk about your personal possessions on the bus or anywhere else. There's always someone who is listening who shouldn't be. I'm so worried about you.'

'Why, my dear, I know everyone in this village.

No one would want my bits and pieces. Besides,' she finished, devastatingly, 'the Gyppos haven't camped in the quarry for years now, so I'm quite safe.'

I tried not to be angry. My heart beat so fast it made me feel ill but I could not speak. She did not know that I was one of those 'Gyppos' but even if she did know, surely it would have made no difference. I was ME, a person who had been helping her for over a year. She often said I was a dear, good girl; not unlike the things my mother had called me when I was young. Would she have changed her attitude if she knew who I was? Truth to tell, I never told anyone who I met in my daily life that I was a Gypsy. Not because I felt shame but because they might be ashamed or embarrassed. But that is something they have to live with. I have no pre-judice against any person, whatever their race or social class. I am against badness, rudeness and cruelty of any sort, but above all I hate injustice. Gypsies as a group suffer terribly from this. It surprises me that all sorts of people use racist-type behaviour against Gypsies with-out reprisal.

Maude's careless chatter on the bus paid off for one non-Gypsy eavesdropper. Maude arrived home one winter afternoon to find her pristine new home had been broken into. All her little treasures had been stolen. Nothing was left of the things she had carefully kept safe for seventy or eighty years. Maude was overcome. All the years that she had felt safe in her own home, leaving her doors unlocked, were over. The culprits were never found. I went to Maude's for several months after but it was all too much. She went into hospital and died shortly after. It crossed my mind that it might have been better to have left things as they were. She was happy and secure in her mice-infested home and then I came along. Although we were told from the start that we had to remember that it was *their* home and we must not interfere, if there was a danger such as a very old appliance or rodent infestation, we had to report it so that it could be sorted out. We did what we had to do. It was a shame that someone stole her keepsakes. She had enjoyed a long life and had loved talking to people. It was part of who she was. Poor Maude. It was more of a shame they had not realised that they had taken much more from her than the objects themselves.

13

Bristly Ox Tongue

I first met Mrs Hardacre on a hot day in early
June. She lived in one of a row of pretty cottages
built for soldiers returning from the Great War
so they could marry the girls that had waited for
them. Although the cottages were small, I was
surprised to see how big her back garden was. She
told me that there was a good reason for this. Most of
the returning soldiers had very little money and the
garden, which was bursting with fruit and vegetables,
was a lifesaver to many young families. I saw her at
the far end of the garden, shaking out some clothes. I
waved to her and she waved back and waited for me
to approach her. She was short, plump and white-
haired and her face was as brown as a berry and very
wrinkled.

'Hello,' I said. 'You look very busy.'

'Yes, I'm just dressing my scarecrow. This year she's
gonna be a lady.'

'Can I help?'

'Yes you can,' she said, handing me a bundle of ladies' clothing.

We dressed the scarecrow between us, which was great fun. This is a good start, I thought, she likes a bit of a joke. I couldn't have been more wrong.

'Wait a second,' she said, picking up a small axe. 'Bring me over that chunk of wood there.'

She pointed to a log with dark stains and motioned for me to fetch it.

'Set it down there, will you?' she said, pointing at a paving slab. I obeyed and watched her open a little gate in the side of the chicken run. The hens all thought they were going to be fed and bustled up together, clucking away happily. Suddenly, she lunged forward and grabbed a plump brown hen.

'That'll make a good meal,' she said, prodding the hen's breast. With a quick movement she wrung the bird's neck. To say I was shocked was an understatement. I felt sick and acid burned in my throat. Worse was to come. Handing me the still-warm chicken and the axe, she pointed to the chopping block. That's what it was, I thought.

'Cut its 'ead off, quick,' she said, shutting the gate.

'But it's already dead,' I gasped.

'I bleed my fowls. The meat is clean then.' She made to walk away.

'Come back, Mrs Hardacre. I'm not supposed to do this sort of thing. I'm not a butcher!'

'I know that. It's not hard,' she grumbled. Snatching the bird from my shaking hand, with a swift movement she flung it on the chopping block and decapitated it before me. The blood flowed and the sickening smell filled the air. I turned quickly and walked back up to the cottage and waited at the gate.

'I s'pose you ain't s'posed to pluck 'em neither.'

I made no reply and she showed me into her cottage. I had never seen such a barren house. No radio. No TV. Only four books on an otherwise empty bookshelf, which had been Sunday school prizes. No flowers, pictures or photographs. There was an old fashioned settee which was faded almost white, two matching armchairs and faded curtains. The gas fire looked ancient as well. The floor was covered in old linoleum and a rag rug. The kitchen was a good size and easily took a large table and four chairs, a new gas cooker (which she told me had been provided free by the gas company due to conversion to natural gas), two cupboards and a sink unit. The whole cottage was exceptionally clean but totally bare and comfortless. The fact that it was so clean made no difference. I was still expected to take outside whatever could be moved, dust under the chairs and scrape any residue from the chair legs, polish the lino on my hands and knees, vacuum the hall carpet and shake all the threadbare rugs outside, all of which was completely unnecessary. She kept her eye on me, all the time complaining about the 'girls of today' being lazy.

The stairs led out of the living room. They were very steep, narrow and uncarpeted, just painted.

'I'll show you upstairs,' she said. I followed her slowly up each precarious step. There were two bedrooms, both as bare and comfortless as downstairs.

'I'll show you what to do,' she said, lifting the coverlets on the bed, 'vacuum the spare room, dust the bed springs and polish the headboard and shake the mats.'

Why? I thought to myself. She had been allocated six hours a week and I could have done everything necessary in an hour. Many people really needed more help and were allocated less. She chattered as she watched me comply with her list of jobs.

'I'm ninety-two. I didn't marry until my forties. I brought up a stepdaughter too. She never visits me. Neither does my granddaughter.'

As I got to know her, this did not surprise me. She had no friends, just acquaintances with whom she gossiped on every occasion. She never knew that I was a Gypsy but I am sure that she had guessed because of some of the pointed remarks she made.

'I've had these pegs for years,' she said, with a knowing look. 'Real Gypsy pegs. They do last.'

'Fancy,' I remarked. I could see at a glance that the pegs she showed me had never been anywhere near a Gypsy. Her personal remarks could be a bit upsetting. She constantly chided me on one matter.

'You haven't dusted my vacuum cleaner.' I found this remark ridiculous. Then she would give me a black look and say, 'I don't know what your own home must be like!'

I ignored this for a long time until one day she made the same remarks followed by, 'I'm ninety-two!' She did look good for her age, I must say. I looked her straight in the face.

'I suppose you think that your great age gives you the right to make impertinent remarks to me. It's only my good manners that prevent me from answering you in the same way!'

She just stared back in silence but she did have the grace to blush. I had not finished with her though. The next day I brought a packet of photos of the interior of my home, which is very clean and comfortable with rugs, books and fresh flowers on the table. It is nothing out of the ordinary, but homely. I chose the best of these and a few of my children on days out or in the garden with their friends. I took them out of my bag and placed them on her kitchen table before I went out shopping for her.

'Can I leave these here, while I'm out? I don't want to lose them,' I said casually.

'Yes, of course.'

'You can have a look at them if you like,' I said as I went out of the door. I was gone about twenty minutes. When I walked in she was still leafing through the photos. I put her shopping away and waited for her to comment.

'Very nice pictures,' she said. 'Whose home is that?'

'Oh, that's mine.'

'Is it?' she said, surprised. 'It's very posh!'

'Oh no. It's not at all. I couldn't live in a house I couldn't relax in.'

'I suppose these were taken when you had just moved in.'

'No, that was taken quite recently. I am very particular about cleanliness and hygiene. I have to be with four school-aged children. We have lots of visitors and I work so I have to look after it well.'

It seemed to dawn on her that her remarks about my cleanliness were far from the truth. The prejudice I had been subjected to for a large part of my life had made me just a little sensitive to the thought that because of my background I must live in some kind of squalor. That made me all the more determined to prove my point. I would like to say that she never made spiteful remarks to me again but that would not be true. However, she did make them less often. I bumped into her previous home help some time after when I was shopping in town.

'Sorry you got landed with Mrs Hardacre,' she apologised.

'What do you mean?'

'The time I spent with her got me down so much I asked to be moved. I called those days my "penance days!"'

'Why?' I laughed.

'I wondered what wrongs I must have committed in a previous life to be punished like that!'

'But she's always telling me what a wonderful worker you were and that she wishes she could have you back!' I gasped. I told her about what I had done with the photos.

'I don't blame you,' she said, 'I did get to tell her what I really thought of her the day I left, though. I told her I was leaving because I was on the edge of a nervous breakdown. Her house was making me depressed and it was the most miserable house I had ever been in.

She threatened to report me. I said, "Please do!" I don't know if she did or not.'

'I don't think so. I never heard anything,' I said.

Thank goodness people like that are few and far between. Like many of 'my ladies' she died alone and left all her money to people who never bothered with her when she was alive.

What a contrast my next new client was! The day was warm and sunny and the garden of the house I had been sent to was full of flowers. Ha! I thought, I'm going to love it here. She was a beautiful West Indian lady. I felt welcome as soon as I saw her wide smile and the open door. She was dressed colourfully with large gold ear-rings and a dazzling smile. Her name was Florence and it suited her very well. She welcomed me into her home with a cup of tea and a biscuit. She did not look at all elderly but the worksheet information said she was seventy-nine.

'This is a lovely day,' she said. 'The Lord has been *most* kind.'

I could not help smiling at her; she made my heart feel glad. Her little house was spotless and as bright as she was. When I asked her what she wanted me to do for her, she caught hold of my hand and looked into my face earnestly.

'I want you to help me pack, my dear. I am going home. I have been told that the time I have left is short and although I have lived here many years, I need to have my last sleep with my parents. I have no one here who is family. I do have many friends but I have made all my arrangements so that no one will have to worry about me.'

'I'm sure no one would call you a worry,' I smiled. 'Where's home?'

'Jamaica!' she said, nodding to a postcard on her sideboard.

All morning I helped her sort and pack the few things she wanted to take with her. The rest went into boxes for charity. I noticed her pieces of furniture had labels with the names of the people she wanted to leave them to. When we had finished everything that could be done she made another cup of tea.

'I hope that I will be able to purchase my special brand of tea,' she said. 'It has always been a joy to sit with a friend and have a cup of tea.'

'I've only just met you, Florence,' I smiled, 'but you make me feel like a friend!'

'It took many years for me to settle here and I met many people who I would not call friends but my parents always told me, "if they treat you good, then you be glad. If they treat you bad, do not show that you hurt, but treat them better." That is why today I have many good friends and it's why I love England so much.' She lowered her eyes. 'But I must go home to be with my parents.'

'I can see how much you long to go home but I do wish I had known you sooner,' I said, squeezing her hand.

'You are obviously a young woman who sees people for who they are.' I was struck by her beautiful English accent and remarked on it.

'When I first came to England, I worked for a lovely English woman. I was very young but I so wanted to speak correctly, so I copied my mistress as best as I could. One day, she said to me, "Florence, who is teaching you to speak so well? Who is your teacher?" I said, "Madam, you are my teacher. I try to speak as you speak." For a minute, she could not reply. I was thinking that she was cross with me! Then she said, "Well, Florence. I am honoured that you chose me to be your teacher."' She paused and smiled. 'I stayed for many years with that family. I always felt that I had been blessed.'

'I think you would have been happy wherever you went, Florence,' I said.

'One day, I was serving lunch to one of my mistress's friends,' she continued, 'and I answered her most politely. "Well, Florence," she said, "if I only heard your voice, I could swear you were a white girl!" My mistress looked sad but after the meal she spoke to me quietly. She said, "Take no notice of ignorant remarks, Florence." I should have told that lady that I had a wonderful teacher.'

I knew exactly what Florence was talking about but I did not say how. I learned a lot about people from my conversations with my ladies. I remembered the wonderful way my mother had taught me how people view things differently but what the truth of the matter really was.

When I had been very young, I had hardly seen a black man or woman. The war had changed all that and we saw more people from far-off places when they began to settle here. I overheard someone telling my cousins that if you touched a black person, the colour wore off. I thought this very strange and, suspecting that it was not true, I went to inquire of my mother who was baking in the wagon.

'No, of course not,' she said, 'that is the colour of their skin. It never comes off, just as your skin colour doesn't come off.'

'Why are people's skin different colours though?'

'It's how we were born. We're all different. No one looks exactly the same do they?' And she added, 'Just remember, it's not the colour of your skin, or what you look like on the outside that makes you who you are. It's how you are on the inside that counts. We are all the same inside.'

I must have looked perplexed because she sat me down on the bench and showed me three eggs from her basket. One was pearly white, one dark brown and one was speckled and creamy.

'Look, what colour are these eggs?' she asked. I carefully described each one's shell in turn.

'Do you see the difference?'

'Yes,' I nodded. She took a glass bowl and broke each one into it, one at a time. Smiling, she handed me the bowl.

'Now, what I want you to do is show me which egg is which.'

I stared into the bowl. Three yellow yolks swirled around in it but which was which?

'I don't know. They all look the same.'

'That's right! We are all the same inside. We show

others what we are like by the way we treat them and by the way we behave. Either good or bad.'

My mother taught me this when I was no more than five years old and I have always remembered it and so taught all my children. Except, being clever, they asked me what Mum had done with the eggs. Were they scrambled or fried?

I remember taking Sarah down to the beach one day when she was around three. She loved it because there was often a child or other children to play with. The beach was almost deserted when we arrived one morning. It was already warm and the tide was still in. Another mum had sat down a short distance from us, and our children soon found each other and played together happily all morning – her beautiful, curly-haired black son and my beautiful blonde-haired daughter. Eventually it started to get too hot so I called her back.

'It's time to go home, Sarah!' I called. She came back very reluctantly.

'Say goodbye to your little friend,' I said. She turned to her little playmate and said goodbye. Then she turned to his mother and said: 'Hasn't he got a lovely tan?'

I never had a camera to record that beautiful moment but it is as clear as crystal in my memory and a testament to my mother's lesson.

14

Dog Daisies

We home helps were sometimes sent to clients temporarily while they were waiting to be assigned a permanent help. I was told to go to a lady who was healthy but a bit forgetful. She lived in a block of flats, three storeys up, together with several cats. According to my worksheet, the neighbours had been complaining about the smell of cats' wee in the stairwell. The smell in the stairwell was bad but nothing like the odour that greeted me as my client opened her door. I tried to introduce myself while holding my breath. I can tell you that it cannot be done.

'Hello, I'm Rosemary, your temporary home help,' I said, red in the face and gasping for breath.

'Oh, thank you, thank you. Come in. As you can see, I'm very tidy.'

Actually, in spite of the smell, this was true. Her home was immaculate but the smell of cat urine was so strong that my eyes were streaming and my throat became sore. The old lady seemed to be immune to it. I asked where the cats did their toilet.

'Oh,' she said airily, pointing, 'I lets 'em out on the balcony. They've got a dirt tray.'

Suddenly a large, black tomcat snuggled into a cushion and urinated. I could hear him. Obviously the old lady could not. Either that or she did not care. There were cats everywhere. I tried counting them but they were running about. I estimated about fifteen. I had no idea how I was going to help her get rid of them. She very kindly offered me a cup of tea but I had to refuse. There were cats on her worktops sniffing the cups and I could not face drinking from one of them even though they looked spotless. I was afraid to sit down, not knowing if they had recently used the soft furnishings as a toilet.

'My front bedroom needs bottoming,' she suggested when I asked her where she would like me to start. Lucky me, I thought. I knew what she meant. I went into the bedroom, which was pleasantly odour free. I opened the window and sniffed gratefully at the clean air. She followed me in and promptly closed it.

'Sorry, I need the window open or I will … start coughing,' I said, resisting the urge to say 'be sick'.

She reopened the window but I could tell she would have preferred it closed.

'If you could strip the bed and vacuum the mattress for me?' she asked and left me to it. I whipped off the blankets and suddenly the room was full of floating money. Five-pound notes, tens and twenties were all whirling around. I stared in disbelief as my client came in and gazed with me. I started chasing the notes.

'What's going on?' she asked. 'Is that yours?'

'No, of course not. It's yours. It's certainly not mine.'

'Where did it all come from then?' she said, picking up a large handful of notes.

'You must have put it under your mattress for safe keeping and forgotten about it.'

After she had calmed down, I asked her if there was someone she could ring to help her sort out what to do with it all. She rang a friend who came round quickly and helped her to remember why she had not put it into the bank.

'You didn't trust the banks, you said,' her friend explained gently. 'You told me you had a safe place to put it. That must be more than a year ago, though. I had forgotten all about it 'til now.'

'Oh, yes, I do remember now,' said my cat lady. She left me alone with her friend while she went to put the kettle on. As soon as she had left the room, the friend tugged my sleeve and begged me to get rid of the cats and the furniture that was ruined.

'We'll have to stick together on this,' I said thoughtfully. 'We will have a cup of tea with her – no need to drink it – and I will explain how unhealthy this all is. If you back me up I'm sure she will see the sense of it.'

Her friend agreed. I told the cat lady that if she continued to own so many cats she would become very ill and then the cats would be all alone. Much better to re-home them now and perhaps just keep one. She allowed herself to be persuaded and so I made a beeline for the chair that I had seen in most recent use. When I removed the cushion cover it literally leaked cat urine onto the floor. I rang the office and arranged for the carpets and furniture to be removed and the flat had to be fumigated. Even as someone who loved cats as much as she did, she had to admit it was a dreadful mess. She was able to buy new furnishings for her flat as the forgotten savings she had discovered came to more than two thousand pounds. This was the early seventies when this amount went a long way. When everything was clean and fresh and new homes had been found for the other cats we stood and looked around her flat. Her friend had come round to see and she admired the new sofa and armchair.

'Well,' I said, 'what do think of your new home now?'

'Thank you, both. I love it!' she smiled. 'Now, perhaps you'll both have a cup of tea with me.' We did so and the one little cat she had kept went to sleep in front of the fire.

On the way home my thoughts flew back to when I was a small child. We had had dogs and cats. Granny herself had been very fond of animals but firmly believed that their place was outside in the little homes we had made for them in the wash-house. They were allowed to wander inside in the daytime but were banished to their own quarters at night. As for allowing them to roam over tables and chairs that we used, that was definitely not allowed and the animals knew it too. I felt exactly the same. The very thought of eating or drinking out of a cup or plate that a pet had eaten from turned my stomach. I had even seen my mother deliberately smash a saucer from a set she had loved after a visiting gadje had poured tea into it and placed it at their feet for one of the dogs to lap up. She had glanced knowingly at my father first and then allowed it to slip from her grasp to the ground with a crash. None of us would have wanted to use it again after that. It would have been showing disrespect to a visitor to even think of giving them the same china the cats and dogs had eaten from. No, pets were loved and looked after but they were taught to know their place. During all my years as a home help I often saw cats and dogs use china that was then given to visitors. I wondered what my grandparents would have said if they had known this.

I loved animals as I had been brought up with them, but I was taken aback when I met Pearl and her dog. One Saturday I received a work slip in the post. My new client was a lady with very little sight. She lived in a first-floor flat overlooking fields and she had a border collie. That's lovely, I thought, remembering my little collie, Tiny. When I arrived, I was met by a short plump lady who seemed pleasant. The first thing she wanted me to do was change the bed. That was fine except the sheets and blankets were threadbare.

'Do you know of any bedding going spare?' she asked. 'You know, from someone who's passed away?'

Hang on a minute, I thought, I've only been here five

minutes. Actually, I often came by bedding and curtains or other household items that were shared among those in need. I had only been with Pearl a short time but I already had a good idea of what to expect.

'Mind you,' she added, 'I want them all washed and aired!'

'But of course,' I said dryly. I wondered who she thought was going to wash and air said blankets and curtains.

Her dog, which was old and scruffy, needed grooming badly and shed hair over everything.

'The living room next,' she ordered. I wondered why I felt so out of place. The room was comfy except for all the dog hair. Then I noticed that there were no pictures, flowers, books; not even a nodding dog. She did have a radio and a small television. I asked her why she had no pictures or plants in the room. I should have realised why.

'Why should I? I can't see them can I?'

'No, but others who visit you can and your room would look so nice with a few home comforts.'

'I don't worry about others. I don't get any visitors anyway.'

She told me that she couldn't see things but I was unsure of that. I did get the impression that she could see a lot more than she let on. Time would tell. Meanwhile, the poor dog, whose name was 'Dog', continued to shed all over the flat. This made me sneeze constantly.

'What's the matter with you?' she asked. 'You seem to have a constant cold.'

'It's not a cold, it's the dog hair,' I sniffed.

'There's a brush under the sink. You can take her onto the balcony and give her a good brush.'

'It's not my job to groom your dog. Besides, her feet and teeth need a bit of attention. Her coat is very dry and I'm sure she's almost blind in one eye.'

When I went a few days later, Dog had been groomed, her poor feet had been sorted and her teeth had been attended to. Nothing could be done about her blind eye but she looked so much better. The vet had made sure that Pearl knew that Dog had to be properly fed.

'It costs me pounds!' she moaned.

'Well at least Dog won't shed so much,' I said. 'Her hair gets into everything. The teacups were full of it this morning. It's not healthy.'

'Oh, all you ever say is "It's not healthy", well, it's never harmed me!'

'Well, I don't want it in *my* tea thank you!' I said firmly. I had a dog but I never found hairs in my food or cups of tea. To be fair, she did feed Dog better than she had done before. Her coat improved and one day when I was in town, I bought a very nice grooming brush. If I had time for a cup of tea before leaving I would give Dog a good brush, which she obviously enjoyed. There was still a lot of shed hair on the carpets and floating in the air.

One morning, about six weeks before Christmas, I arrived to find she had got out butter, flour and all that was needed for a rich fruit cake. She assured me she could weigh it all out and she proceeded to grease the tins. To my horror, I realised that as she did this she was rubbing Dog's hair in as well.

'Stop, Pearl. The grease is full of dog hair. It's unhealthy.' I took the tins from her and threw them in the sink with plenty of hot water and washing-up liquid. She was very angry with me.

'I'm making this cake for a friend! I always give her a cake.'

'Right then. I'll grease your tins and weigh your ingredients. I can't stand by and watch you greasing tins and mixing flour and butter with dog hair floating around.'

'She's never complained to me before. She loves my cake!'

I looked her in the eye. I was going to say, how would *you* like it? But I refrained, thinking she must have eaten pounds of the stuff. She gave in and let me grease the tins. I also made sure all her utensils were spotless. That was the best I could do. She showed me the cake the following week and it looked and smelled delicious. Well, I thought, I've done my best. There was still masses of dog hair everywhere. I swept up swathes of it on the tiled kitchen and bathroom floors. I gave up complaining about it.

'What would you like me to buy you for Christmas?' she asked me one morning.

'Nothing at all, thank you Pearl. I don't even buy presents for my extended family. I have everything I need. Please don't spend your money on me.'

I knew what was going on. She had been hinting for weeks that she was very hard up and could not even afford to buy herself the pair of thick woolly tights that she had seen in the local draper's window. I heard this often. She was always saying that she was hard up.

'Aren't we all?' was my usual reply as I wondered how we were going to pay the gas bill. I was having two weeks off for the holiday and on the last morning at Pearl's she handed me a carrier bag.

'What is it?' I asked suspiciously.

'It's for you.' She stood there smiling expectantly, waiting for me to give her the red tights, I supposed.

'Pearl, I told you not to give me any gifts. We aren't allowed to accept *anything* at all from our clients,' I sighed. 'Enjoy your holiday,' I said as I left. She had managed to make me feel bad about it. I am not a mean person at all. I often accepted little treats such as home-made cake or a posy of wild flowers, or I took some of their heavy washing home. I did this for all my ladies because I wanted to and I know some of my colleagues did the same, but none of us wanted to be put on the spot or cajoled into anything. On arriving home, I put the kettle on. John came in a few minutes later.

'I can't stop. I've only got five minutes for a cuppa and a piece of cake.'

I opened the bag. There, wrapped in foil was a cake!

'Oh no,' I groaned.

'What's up?' John asked. I pointed into the bag and he peered into it at what looked like a beautiful rich fruit cake.

'That looks good,' he said, 'that'll go down well with my tea.'

He caught my eye and I started to laugh until I cried. John had picked up a knife from the drawer.

'I'll cut myself a piece,' he said.

'No, no!' I gasped. 'Don't!'

'Why? Are you keeping it, then?'

I mopped the tears from my eyes. 'No, I'm not!' Bending over the cake, I started pulling long hairs out of it and soon there was a pile on the table and the cake had quite a furry appearance.

'Is it for the animals?' said John, gaping at it.

'No, it's a special cake for me, with all the best ingredients and one added extra – dog hairs!'

While I had been with other clients, Pearl had made me a cake. We certainly could never eat it. I fed it to the seagulls who were not so fussy and they did away with it in seconds. I could not help thinking that it would have been more sensible if she had bought her own red tights.

When I went back after the holiday she never said a word but continued to give me reproachful looks. On the Wednesday morning, we had a Home Help's Bring and Buy Sale in order to support our local hospice. Before we started we had a cuppa and a chat, exchanging little jokes and stories about the people we helped, no names mentioned. One of my colleagues had me in fits when she told us all about the lady whose home was covered in dog hair and who had asked her to help her make a rich fruit cake for her usual home help.

'I didn't know what to do for the best,' she laughed. 'Everything was covered in dog's hair. I did mention it to her and she just said ...'

I joined her in finishing her sentence and we both said in unison: '*It never hurt me!*'

'Oh, no,' she gasped. 'It was for *you*!'

I was shocked by the way Pearl treated Dog. I believe that if you have charge of an animal it is up to you to take care of it. As children, we often had little squabbles over whose turn it was to bath, brush or feed our animals but we did love to brush Granny's Persian cat. Her fur was a soft, bluish grey and her eyes were green. She did not have a proper name; we just called her 'Pusscat' and she always answered to this. Her fur was brushed every day to keep it free from knots.

'Don't fergit 'er belly,' Granfer would say, 'but don't 'ee touch 'er tender spot. She'll go fer 'ee if 'ee do!'

That was true. She was as gentle as could be but there was one small spot on her belly that she could not bear to be touched. If we went near it we always knew because her body would tense and her eyes would dilate until they were an angry black. Just before that happened, we knew when to stop. Granny bought her collar after collar with her name and address on. We would groom her and then put on her new collar. Pusscat would stroll off to find a sunny spot and within a few seconds, the collar would be off. She would then scoop it up in her strong teeth and run off to hide it; who knows where because none of them were ever found.

'Mary Ann!' Granfer would gently scold, 'Don't 'ee waste thy vonger. Pusscat just don't like they collars!'

'Yes my Edwin. I knows that but I keeps 'opin',' she would reply. We children would hunt for a nest of cat collars for Granny but we never did find one.

My cousin Violet had a ginger and white tomcat that she called by the fanciful name 'Chico' after a character she had seen in a film. She adored this cat and treated it like a baby, washing its face after meals and only giving it the best food. One day when she was at school, Chico got run over while crossing the road. Of course she was broken-hearted and would not be comforted with another. There were always cats and dogs around and the horses were always brushed, fed and watered, Granfer saw to that. It was never a chore, it was a pleasure.

All of our animals were loved and cared for. Maybe there was no tinned food to be had but there were always the leftovers and plenty of them. Whenever we had rabbit stew or a chicken was killed the pets benefited. Granny would ask for bones at the butchers and all of the animals ate vegetables mixed in with their food. An animal is not fussy. My father always said that it was eating vegetables as well as meat that made all of our animals so gentle and gave them such shiny coats. He was often heard to say: 'Give that poor cat (or dog) a bit o' peace. He's been brushed enough for one day!'

One of the most frightening things that ever happened to me occurred while I was a home help; it did not scare me at the time, but in retrospect it was terrifying. The weather had been very cold for early October but I was still surprised when my knock at the front door of a new client caused it to be opened by what appeared to be a bundle of woollies.

'Come in quick, gel!' said a voice from the bundle. A

hand appeared from within, grabbed me by the arm and tugged me inside.

'Good morning, Mrs Ware ...' I began, but she shut me up.

'Yes, yes I know. You be from the council. I wants you to look at my fire. It won't light.'

She opened a door and straight away I could smell gas.

'Phew!' I gasped. 'Open the window!'

'No, don't!' she argued. 'It's too dang cold!'

'We'll be a dang sight colder if we don't open the windows and the doors!'

'Why?'

'Why do you think?' I said, flinging open the living room window. 'We'll be gassed!'

'Oh,' she said sniffing, 'I can smell it but it ain't too bad.'

I opened all the doors and windows and once the fumes had dispersed a bit I rang the emergency gas service. When I walked back into the living room, to my shock and utter horror, the old lady knelt by the gas fire, took a box of matches from the mantelpiece and prepared to strike one. I was furious. I snatched the matches from her hand and threw them straight through the open window.

'What on earth are you doing?' I shrieked.

'For goodness sake! I was only going to run them under the pipe to see if there was a leak,' she grumbled. I just shook my head in silence.

'I've turned off the mains. You should have done that at once or got someone else to do it for you.'

There was a noise outside and then the gas men rushed in. Seeing we were safe, they relaxed. I suddenly noticed the budgie cage and two little clawed feet sticking upwards.

'One casualty,' I said, nodding towards the cage.

'Oh! My poor little Dinkie! He's dead!' Mrs Ware squealed.

'Just be glad it wasn't *you*, Mrs Ware,' I said.

'Go outside for a bit while we make sure everything is safe for you,' said one of the gas men. A neighbour had come out to see what the commotion was about and kindly took us into her house. She was so shocked.

'My house could have gone up in flames!' she gasped. After a cup of tea she spoke to me quietly.

'She's not safe, you know. She does all sorts of silly things,' she whispered confidentially. The gas man called us back.

'I don't know how on earth you've survived. The fire's lethal and must not be used again. I've put a warning label on it. The pipes are so old they've cracked,' he said. 'The house was full of gas. The only thing that's saved you is the draughts!'

'Yes, the house is draughty,' I agreed. 'She hasn't been using her cooker because she has meals on wheels and she keeps all her doors open.'

'The budgie died because it's so small but even so, you've both had a very lucky escape.' He turned to look gravely at Mrs Ware.

'All's well that ends well,' she said casually.

'Mrs Ware, you may be taking this lightly but I certainly don't!' I snapped. 'You might be in your eighties but I am in my early forties. I don't expect to take my life in my hands every time I knock on someone's door! This has been a very frightening experience for me.'

'I'm sorry my dear. I don't expect you to do any cleaning today. I'll ring for a taxi and we will buy a new budgie,' she smiled and added, 'I'll get one for you too if you like.'

'Thank you, but I would never keep an animal or a bird in a cage.'

'Oh, well. There's nowt so queer as folk.'

This philosophy I heartily agreed with.

Mrs Ware was moved to a smaller home soon after, which we all hoped would be safer for her. It was warden controlled and all electric. I only went to her a few times after that. She showed me her new budgie. He was quite a chatterbox. He had learned a few phrases and told me to 'hang up your hat dear' and 'get mum a cup of tea' which was quite funny the first few times but palled after a few dozen.

No, I could never keep an animal in a cage. How desperate they must feel seeing freedom just outside the bars and yet not able to attain it. My cousin Johnny had felt the same. His tears flowed as he cried to his teachers about his beloved jackdaw.

''E loves me, Miss. I can't put 'im in a cage!'

Freedom is such a wonderful thing for all, human or animal alike. As children we had it in abundance. It is a very lovely thing to wake up to a new day and know that no money would be needed to enjoy the simple pleasures of wandering the fields, picking flowers, hedgerow fruit and nuts, paddle in warm shallow river water and, when your belly gives you a nudge, run home and sit with your family to enjoy a steaming plate of rabbit stew.

15

Lily of the Valley

O ne Saturday morning I received a note in the post from Mrs Jordan giving me the name and details of my next new client. She was to have two hours on Monday and two hours on Thursday. She lived only a few minutes' walk from my home so I would not have to leave until 8.45 in the morning. All of my four children had gone off to school so it was nice not to feel rushed that Monday. It was a warm spring day when I first met Lily. I found her in her back garden among the daffodils. She did not look up when I approached but was deeply engrossed in some activity. She stopped and I could see a tiny white-haired old lady struggling with a spade that was almost as big as she was. It was clear that she was trying to dig up a wayward fuchsia bush.

'Come on yer silly Divil! Git out of it!' she grunted.

'Hello. What are you doing?'

She stood up and rested on her spade. Watching her, I thought, I hope she isn't going to ask me to dig up that bush. She smiled at me as she recognised my uniform.

Usually, I wore my own clothes to work and changed in my clients' homes. My first uniform was navy with white piping, rather like a nurse's.

'Just in time, me dear! There's another spade in the shed. And you can call me Lily.'

I looked her in the eye.

'Oh, no,' I said. 'Gardening is against the rules. I do housework or shopping but no gardening I'm afraid.'

'What?' she exclaimed. 'That's the very thing I wanted help for!'

'Perhaps you should hire a gardener,' I suggested.

'Hmph! The last gardener I had dug up every bulb and plant I owned and sold them to his mates! He was only happy if every bed was dug over and left like a new grave! He cut the grass so short it died!'

By now I was laughing, she was so amusing.

'That was five years ago. I've always done me own gardening since. It's cheaper in the end.'

'Well, if you get one to come while I'm here on Monday or Thursday mornings,' I suggested, 'I'll keep an eye out for you and make sure he doesn't dig anything up.'

'I'll have to think it over,' she said, leaving the spade and hobbling into the house. 'Come and have a cuppa. Then you can start work.'

She led me into her tidy kitchen and, to my surprise, filled a blackened saucepan with water.

'Put some milk, sugar and mugs onto a tray by the sink and come into the front room.' Puzzled, I obeyed as I watched her carry the saucepan into the front room. I followed her through and placed the tray on a small table. Turning, I saw her kneeling in front of an open fireplace. I stared in horror as she put a match to the paper and sticks in the grate. It set alight instantly and she pushed the saucepan deep into the heart of the fire.

'There!' she said. 'That shouldn't take too long to boil.'

I was speechless. I looked around and saw her bed on one side of the room with her commode next to it and a couple more saucepans on another small table containing food, which she was obviously intending to heat up on the open fire for her lunch. I still could not believe my eyes when I saw her crouching to pour the boiling water into the teapot on the grate, spilling some as she did so. My thoughts raced as I quietly sat with her and drank my tea, which had little black smuts floating in it. Staring into the fire and sipping the brown liquid, I spoke without thinking.

'This is a good cup of tea, Lily. It reminds me of the dark brown cups of tea that Granfer used to make on the campfire. It was so strong, I had to take three spoons full of sugar! I can still taste it now. I felt very privileged to sit and drink one of Granfer's wonderful cups of tea on a warm spring morning just like this.'

I suddenly remembered where I was and I looked up to see Lily watching me closely. I wondered what she must have been thinking.

'You was a lucky gal,' she said, 'and what's more, you knew you was lucky.'

'I did indeed,' I agreed, 'but what I want to know, Lily, is why you are using an open fire to boil water and to cook on? You must realise how dangerous that is.'

'Oh no. I'm used to it. I used to do it this way all the time when I was a gal and I lived in the farm cottage with me Mam and Dad.'

'Yes, but times have changed. You needn't be living like this. Don't you have a kettle or a cooker?' I went back through to the kitchen. An ancient cooker stood redundant in a corner. The kettle was broken. Her fridge had apparently kept icing up and then melting suddenly, flooding the kitchen. She had resorted to heating up tinned food on the fire. Her toilet was blocked so she was using a commode.

We had just come through a bitter winter and fuel prices had rocketed. There had been an advertising campaign on TV informing the elderly how to keep warm and well fed but Lily appeared to be living in poverty. I unblocked her toilet myself and cleaned it before ringing the office. At least the telephone worked.

'I'm getting some help for you Lily,' I explained after coming off the phone. 'May I see your pension book?'

She handed it to me. Immediately I could see that Lily had somehow slipped through the net. I knew for certain that she was only receiving a quarter of the allowance she was entitled to. How could this happen? I learned that she had a wonderful daughter-in-law who did a lot for her. They had just both accepted what she was receiving in ignorance. Straight away, I set the ball in motion. Several phone calls later she had a new gas cooker. Her fridge, which was only a few months old, was returned and replaced. It had a faulty thermostat. I threw out her faulty kettle and got her a new one. Within a few months, she had her heating back on and her bed was put back into her bedroom. I had discovered that if I asked the Social Services for help on behalf of my clients, it was always given. The icing on the cake was when Lily received her full entitlement for her pension and benefits. She cried when she showed me her letter, which also informed her that she would get all the back money that was owing to her.

'Now I will be able to buy me grandchildren presents without worrying that I can't afford it!' she sighed. The sad thing was that every time she had a small rise in her benefits after that, she worried in case it was a mistake and she would be asked for it back. Dear Lily, I was so glad that I knew her.

She told me some of her story over the years that I was with her. What a wonderful woman she was. She was in her late eighties when I first met her, with a few physical problems. How she coped with them sometimes, it was hard to understand. She was a happy person, though, and I always felt the happier for seeing her. I still have the fuchsia bush she dug up for me. Now it has at least half a dozen siblings because of the cuttings I took from it.

One thing I discovered with Lily, soon after meeting her, was that she always seemed so sleepy. She would drop off to sleep in mid-sentence sometimes or almost drop a cup of tea as she nodded off. I came across a box of very strong sedatives in the bathroom and several empty boxes. I was shocked. From personal experience, I was aware that this drug should only be taken for the short-term, not for the length of time that she had evidently been taking it.

'Lily, I'm going to ring the surgery for you. Something is not quite right here with your tablets.'

'Oh, dear,' she quavered. 'What have I done? Something wrong?'

'Don't worry, Lily,' I reassured her, 'I'll sort it out.'

Someone from the surgery came immediately and took the pills away. She was taken off the drug slowly and rarely fell asleep suddenly again. Because of this she was more alert and began telling me the story of her life. What an amazing woman! She was nineteen when she met the man who became her husband. They had bought their first home together when the war intervened. Lily was left to try and pay the mortgage and give birth to her first child alone, a son. Times were hard for everyone then but Lily was very careful with her supplies and often a neighbour would pop in for the loan of some tea, sugar or sundry items. Being a good manager, she decided to sell some of these items instead of lending. Soon, she had a nice little business going from her front room. After a time, she said she felt lonely so she put her house up for rent and moved in with her mother and father. She took a part-time job and with the income from her small business she did very well. During the war she only saw her husband two or three times but had become pregnant with her second son. After the war, Lily and her husband had decided to sell up and buy a larger house near her parents.

'I was sitting in my garden, when I had a brainwave!' Lily said. 'My husband had found it hard to get work after the war. I had a huge front room so I decided to open up a shop! That is what we did. Things were a bit easier in those days and the council agreed as long as we opened up part of it as a Post Office. We decided that would be my husband's job. He would be the Post Master and I would run the grocery side!'

'What a good idea!' I enthused.

'We put shelves up and counters and we found a nice glass case for the cakes and buns; we even had a freezer for ice cream! When we had finished, it was as clean and fresh as human hands could make it. Just before we opened on our first day, I went downstairs first thing to have another look. I stood in the doorway, gloating over me shop and looking forward to opening the doors to me new customers. At least that's what I hoped.'

'Why, what happened?' I asked.

'Well, I picked up a clean cloth and wiped the top of the cake case and then I had to blink twice! I had another look, and there, cuddled in with the Swiss rolls, was a mouse fast asleep!'

We both laughed at this.

'Oh no, I thought. It must have got in while we were busy putting everything on the shelves. We had slid the glass across without noticing Mr and Mrs Mouse inside!' she chuckled. 'I called to my husband, "Come quick!" He laughed when he saw what I was pointing at! He got a box and carefully swept the mouse into it, Swiss rolls and all! "I won't harm it," he said, "I'll set it free when I come to a field." So that's what he did. We set a few traps after that, but we never caught no more, I'm happy to say.'

Lily ran her shop for many years after that and then became pregnant with her third child.

'I so wanted a little daughter. A pretty thing with auburn hair,' she said quietly. It was such a tragedy for Lily though. Her little girl was 'born asleep.' She still grieved for that little girl who was lost to her, but she loved her three grandsons very much and she was lucky enough to have a lovely daughter-in-law called Sue, who loved her. She was very good to Lily. One day when Sue called, I noticed a beam of sunlight caught her hair and turned it to copper. I could not help thinking that Lily had got her red-haired daughter after all.

Yes, Lily's daughter-in-law was a girl in a million. She had her own mother living with her and yet she still had time to take care of Lily. The care she gave them reminded me of the care my Romany family gave each other.

The next time I went to see Lily it was a very hot day. She was my last visit of the day, so there was no rush to get finished.

'Let's sit outside in the shade,' Lily suggested. We still had a cup of tea. Lily preferred it to a cold drink. I remarked on her pretty daughter-in-law and how I had noticed her hair sparkling copper red in the sunlight.

'I always wanted a red-haired daughter,' she sighed softly.

'It looks as though you have one,' I said.

'You know, I've never looked at it like that, although I love her dearly. She's better than many daughters.'

I agreed with her completely. Tears filled her eyes.

'I'll never forget my baby girl. I wasn't allowed to touch or hold her. She lay in her shawl like a china doll.

She had been born asleep. Her head was covered in damp golden red tendrils and her cheeks looked fresh and dewy. I loved her at once and I've loved her ever since.'

Tears stung my eyes and a lump came to my throat. I took her gnarled old hand in mine.

'Oh my dear, I do hope I haven't upset you, talking like this!' she said, her eyes widening.

'No,' I replied, squeezing her hand gently. I was remembering my own baby boy. I had told Lily all about him. My second child was a little boy. He looked perfect when he was born with black curly hair and deep blue eyes. But somehow I felt uneasy. He looked deep into my eyes as though he was trying to tell me something. He tried to feed, still gazing into my eyes. In those days the nurses took the babies away between feeds so mothers could rest. When he was brought to me the second time, he was listless. He just lay looking into my eyes as I held him close. I unwrapped his blanket. My heart stood still. His little arm was black. Immediately I rang the bell and a nurse came at once. Wordlessly, I showed her his poor little arm. She took him from my reluctant arms and whisked him out of the ward. I was left alone in the bed with empty arms and an empty heart. Time ticked the afternoon away and I asked a nurse what was wrong with my baby.

'He's just a bit mucousy. I'm sure it's nothing to worry about,' she said briskly. I was left alone once more. I had to wait until John came in after he had finished work to speak to him. He knew nothing of what had happened. He had left me and our new baby with a kiss each the evening before and gone home to tell my mother and little Sarah all about it. He walked into the ward with a smile and a large bouquet.

'John!' I cried. 'Quickly, go and look at our baby! They've taken him away and I think something's wrong.'

His expression changed instantly as he saw mine and he dropped the bouquet and went off to find a doctor. He came back shortly after and tried to console me in the same manner as the nurse had earlier.

'The doctor is worried about him. They've taken him to the children's hospital to be on the safe side and we mustn't worry.'

Mustn't worry? We were in despair. I had not even been told he had left the hospital. We wept silently until I dozed off. I awoke suddenly as though I had been shaken. A nurse stood next to me and explained that my baby had died in the ambulance. He was gone and I never even gave him a last kiss. I never saw him again.

I sometimes wish I had been able to prevent him going in the ambulance and just held him in my arms until he died. Things were different fifty years ago. The hospital report stated that his heart was in a very bad way and nothing could have saved him. He would have been fifty years old this year; fifty years old and yet not old at all. The hole in his poor little heart was not as big as the gaping chasm in my own. I looked up at Lily and smiled.

'I do believe we will see our babies again one day, Lily, and hold them in our arms.'

'What a wonderful day that will be, Rosemary,' she nodded. 'What a wonderful day.'

We were glad to have an extended family who grieved

with us at that time. We did not need counselling. There was always someone there for me to talk to, someone who cared or who had a shared experience. I had only known of the deaths of two babies previously: Aunt Britt's baby girl, Kathleen, and Aunt Rene's baby, Dawn. They are still part of their family life and are talked about as naturally as if they were still present. I think that is the nicest way.

Lily was ninety-two years old and had been grieving for over fifty years and yet she still felt the pain of her loss, even as I do now.

16

Lords and Ladies

abs and Lettice were two sisters who lived in a top-floor flat. The view was wonderful from the flat but neither of them could leave their home to go for a walk or even to the shops. The elder sister was in a wheelchair, but as she said herself, 'What good is that if I can't leave the flat?'

'It won't be long now until you get a ground-floor flat,' I told her.

'We've been waiting so long,' Mabs sighed. 'What a dream day that will be!'

'Well, I'm here to help you pack all the things you don't need for now. I'll put them in the spare room then you'll only have a little left to do on the last day and one or two people will be here to help you then, too.'

'Ooh, we can't wait,' she said with tears in her eyes. 'Come then, where shall we begin? With Mum's old room? We plan to give it all to charity or a jumble sale.'

She took me into a large room and drew back the curtains.

'Goodness!' I exclaimed, 'it's like Aladdin's cave in here!'

Shelves and cabinets were crammed with some amazing things.

'Wow! What a lovely sight! I can't believe my eyes. Some of these things are very valuable you know. You must get them expertly valued.'

'We must sell as many as possible,' said Mabs. 'We have very little money and we need to buy some nice things for our new flat, but those boxes by the door are for the jumble sale. Mum packed them herself.'

'She did say that *her* mother had only paid a few pence for them at the time,' Lettice added.

'That must have been over a hundred years ago then?' I guessed.

'Yes, well over,' said Mabs. I knelt down and opened the first box.

'Well, first we had better look at these.' I unpeeled the wrapping paper and gasped.

'What's the matter?' asked Lettice, leaning over the arm of her wheelchair. 'Wait a moment. I'll spread it out on the bed,' I said to her. I pulled back the heavy curtains a little more and the sun sparkled on the beautiful objects arrayed on the bedcover. Dishes, vases of all sorts, little jugs; the room was full of diamond sparkle. Mabs and Lettice smiled at each other.

'Oh, how pretty!'

Another box was full of hand-cut lead crystal which threw all the colours of the rainbow around the room; red, pink, blue, green, it was just like a wonderland. We all sat gazing at the sight.

'Well!' I said. 'Have you never seen these lovely things before?'

'Oh, no. Mum never had the time or space to display them,' said Mabs.

'Our parents ran a little shop you see,' Lettice interjected. Mabs pointed to some of the glassware.

'Yes, it sold everything from bric-a-brac, ornaments to all sorts of pretty glassware. She often bought from a travelling salesman, didn't she Letty?'

'Oh yes!' Lettice recalled. 'Mum believed all his stories – how he had a sick wife and half a dozen children to support on a meagre wage!'

'And she sold paraffin, candles, knitting wool. All sorts for all sorts as my dad would say,' added Mabs. 'They both worked very hard indeed.'

'Well,' I breathed, 'your mother did very well. There must be at least a dozen pieces of Lalique here. This piece is signed. There's Spode, Crown Derby, Royal Worcester ...'

Mabs squealed in delight.

'Ooh! We watch all the antique shows but I never dreamed of looking in these boxes, did *you* Letty?'

I stood up.

'I know for certain that these bowls are hand-cut lead crystal. Don't touch any of this until you speak with a reputable antiques dealer in town. Ask for a valuation.' I went to fetch the phone book and left the sisters to admire their new-found treasures.

I was present at the valuation and so was a close friend of theirs. The friend was so apologetic.

'The times I've told them to give all this stuff away. I thought it was all rubbish.'

'You didn't know dear,' Mabs said comfortingly.

Her friend showed me a lovely bowl that the sisters had given her.

'But I won't accept it if it's valuable!' she insisted.

'I wouldn't worry,' said the valuer. 'There's more than enough here for what they need!'

I do not know the final sum they received in the end but Mabs and Lettice were overjoyed and their friend kept her bowl. I think she deserved it because she had always been there if they needed help. That is worth more than money to a lonely person. We all helped them move into their lovely little garden flat soon after. They afforded themselves a few luxuries and a few nice holidays. Lettice bought a good electric wheelchair now that they could get out. It made a world of difference to their lives.

'Just think,' said Lettice, 'Mum could have had a maid!'

'Those things may not have had the same value back then but I'm sure your parents would have been over-joyed to know you were so happy,' I smiled. I sat down on my last day with them, drinking the proverbial cup of tea. Mabs put down her cup and stared at me.

'Rosie, you seem very knowledgeable. How could you tell at a glance that most of those things that we thought were worthless were far more valuable than we could ever have imagined?'

Putting my teacup down, I gazed at each of them.

'I could tell you the whole story, but that would take

a lifetime,' I smiled, 'but what I will say is, I am my father's daughter.'

Both my grandparents and my father had an excellent knowledge of antique china, glass and furniture. They were seldom wrong. Dad was not sentimental over possessions. On the other hand, Mum valued things that to others might be completely worthless, simply because of the child or person who gave her the gift. There would not be enough money in anyone's purse to persuade her to part with it. I suppose we are all born with a bit of our ancestors in us. That is what makes us the complex humans that we are. I look back on my childhood and think how blessed we were. Money was no object because we had none. We did not beg our parents for expensive toys, nor feel the loss of not having them because we had never seen advertisements showing these wonders and did not even know they existed. The things we did have were endless hours of sunny days, freedom to make our own fun and close contact with birds and animals. If anything, we took it all for granted. Singing and dancing we had in plenty. If there was anything missing in my life it was books, although my parents tried to give me as many of these as they could, even begging a box of books from the dustman. Reading is my favourite pastime and a gift I will always treasure.

I well remember being left at home with my young cousins who were not much older than I was. We all got together at Aunt Amy and Uncle Fred's place. We were having fun, sharing a huge bowl of nuts. Bobby, Bet's brother, kept dropping shells on the floor and his older sister told him off.

'You ain't me mam!' he called back to Bet, slamming the door. Bet was doing the washing up. In her hand was her mother's cherished crystal sugar bowl. The door slammed at the same moment as a plane passed overhead, making a tremendous noise. It made us all jump. Bet gave a cry of horror. Her mother's precious bowl was broken in two halves. Bet looked shocked.

'It was the plane!' she gasped. Oh dear. What should we do? Bet quickly placed the bowl on the table and pressed the two halves together, and then in a breath she picked up the bag of sugar and filled the bowl. To our astonishment it held together. We all gasped and laughed in a fearful way. Bet put the kettle on and got some cups ready. When Aunt Amy and Uncle Fred came in they were ready for a cuppa. Bobby had come back into the room and Bet gave him his tea first. He reached for the sugar bowl and the look on his face when he realised he was holding half a sugar bowl was a sight to see. Not one of us laughed but all looked suitably shocked and surprised.

'I didn't do it!' said Bobby. None of us said a word. We all made ourselves scarce, gathering together outside, laughing hysterically. A few days later I heard Aunt Amy telling my mother.

'It just broke in 'is 'and, Mary,' she said, 'nobuddy seems to know 'ow it broke. Just broke in 'is 'and.' My mother, knowing nothing, made a suggestion.

'Perhaps the water might have cracked it when you washed up, Amy?'

'Yes it might 'ave.' I never told my mother the truth. I don't know if Aunt Amy ever found out or not. It was a small tragedy. We had very few lovely things so we tended to use them and got pleasure from doing so. The treasured bowl was broken and no one was blamed. I mentioned it to Bet recently and she still believes it was the noise from the plane that caused the breakage. Who knows?

It is very strange how things that you remember from your youth come back to haunt you when you are older. When Granfer trawled the markets he sometimes came home with next to nothing. Other times he would return with a whole cartload of goodies which we children could hardly wait to get our hands on. There would be furniture, pictures or boxes filled with all sorts of everything. Some of it would be junk but there were exciting treasures too. On one occasion he brought home dozens of pictures, many of which were only fit for the fire. The frames of several were worth a lot of money. Granfer kept a couple for Granny's wall in her hut. These were mostly of horses and they looked good hanging either side of the shiny brass horses' hames on the dark wall. One of these was Granfer's particular favourite. It was of two pretty young women all dressed up in their best clothes and picture hats. They were watching two young men in straw hats and blazers trying to get their jalopy started again as they appeared to have broken down on their way to a picnic. Next to them were two beautiful horses hanging their heads over a gate who appeared to be commenting on this scene, and the caption read:

'They'll need us yet!' I read this out to Granfer. He was overjoyed.

'Listen to that, Mary Ann!' he laughed. 'They'll need us yet!' He laughed and laughed over this, slapping his knee and repeating the horses' knowing quip, 'Hah! They'll need us yet!' Granfer always said that two horses were worth a dozen cars. That picture hung on the wall for as long as I can remember. It was probably just a print but what did that matter? Granfer loved it.

The picture I remember most of all was one that frightened me. It gave me such a troubling feeling that I wanted to cry. The sadness of it seemed to jump out of the frame and tendrils of misery wrapped themselves around my person, stroking my face and hair with icy fingers. I did not tell my mother about this at first. I knew she liked it very much as she would sit and look at it whenever she had a few minutes to spare. It was hung on the wall of our wagon in the only space above the range. The picture was of a middle-aged woman with an opened letter in her hand, obviously very distressed and sitting on a big bed next to a beautiful young woman who held her in her arms, comforting her. It must have been a good picture as it felt so real to me I could not bear it. After a while I told my mother that it made me feel miserable. Mum did not say much but the next day I came home from school to find it gone. I was so relieved.

'Granfer sold it for forty pounds,' said Mum. That was a lot of money in 1945. I was just glad it was gone. Many years later, I was sent to a man whose house was crammed with artefacts, pictures, furniture and ornaments. His wife was frail. He was rude to say the least. He also liked everyone to know how well off he was.

'I hope you can keep your mouth shut!' he said, pointing his stick at me.

'I hope that goes without saying,' I replied.

'I wouldn't want the house robbed because the home help talks.'

I was angry at his assumption but I let it pass. His wife was charming and I could see how embarrassed she was. I felt sorry for her. Day after day he boasted about his belongings and how valuable they were. At least I could shut the door and go home. He always stayed in the room when I was cleaning.

'Don't get me wrong,' he said, winking, 'but I don't like to put temptation in the help's way.'

I had had enough of this.

'You may be surprised to know, Mr Peters,' I said icily, 'that I can tell you the price of everything you have. My father and grandfather bought and sold this sort of thing all their lives and mine.' I did not look up from my dusting.

'Really?' he said, looking down his nose at me. 'You haven't seen my paintings. They are very different and exciting, especially the monochromes. You do *know* what monochrome means, I presume? Bring this girl into my art room!' he demanded, glaring at his wife.

I could have said no but I wanted to see what he considered to be art. His wife showed me into a long narrow room and switched on the light and then another switch that turned on the lights above each picture. He had quite a display but I was not impressed. I glanced around. They looked quite boring to me, especially the monochromes. Then my eyes stopped dead. It was that picture. The one that I had always hated. Was it the same one? Surely not. Looking closer, I saw a tiny mark on the frame, like a little bit of black paint. It had no doubt been well cleaned and it looked a little lighter but it was the same one all right. I still felt the same. Cold sweat ran out of my hair and down my neck. My palms were sweaty and I thought I was going to die of misery. I quickly glanced at Mrs Peters, aware that she was watching me. She caught hold of my sweaty palm.

'You feel it too?' she whispered. I nodded. I turned on my heel.

'I've seen enough, thank you. I don't want to see any more.'

'This is a very valuable picture,' he said, 'I know the story. That is the wife and daughter of a man who was shot in the 1914 war. He was a coward. I love it.'

'Well,' I said firmly, 'I don't. When I was a small child I saw this painting hanging on the wall of a Romany wagon. It was sold for forty pounds. That's all it was worth then. I wouldn't give you four pounds for it.'

He stared at me in rage.

'How would *you* know its value?'

'Well, my father and grandfather knew people very well and they were very astute. If they really liked something they would not care if it was worth hundreds of pounds or just a few shillings. What is the point, my father used to say, to know the cost of everything and the value of nothing?'

I went to their home for just a few weeks more until I arrived one morning to find that Mrs Peters had quietly died in the night. I was so shocked. I had no idea that she was so ill. She had hardly complained about anything. She had waited on her husband hand and foot though. He was lost without her.

'I don't know what to do,' he whimpered. 'She did everything.'

I realised that I had never heard him speak her name.

'Yes, she was a gem wasn't she? Women like your wife are very rare. She was pretty, kind and generous and very gentle.'

'I know. I did love her but I never told her so.'

I felt pity for him. He had to go into a care home after that. There was no choice. Everything he possessed had to be sold. He was utterly bereft, poor man. He did not live long afterwards. What on earth was the use of possessions when the most important person in your life is no longer there?

17

Lady's Smock

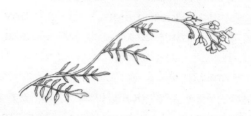

When my cousins and I were small children we
loved all the tiny babies and never tired of
playing with them. If there was a new baby
we would offer to look after it.

'Can we push the baby's pram?' Violet and I would
ask. Or: 'Can we help you hang out the baby's clothes,
Granny?'

Granny would often come home with a basket full of
baby clothes she had begged or bartered for a new baby.

'Yer,' she would say to a new Gypsy mother, 'yers a
few little togs fer the babby.'

Some of these little 'babbies' were really well dressed.
What the gadje babies quickly grew out of, our newborns
benefited from. I loved to see these pretty baby clothes
hanging on the line. One afternoon Granny came home
after a hard day's work, buying and selling.

'Yer Mary,' she said to my mother, 'I bin to a proper
lady today in a big 'ouse. She spoke foreign an' I couldn't
understand a 'alf o' what she said. She was right beautiful

though and she gimme a cuppa tea! She was right smart with a black frock an' a white frilly pinny!'

Mum told me later that this must have been the maid.

'She 'ad a lovely little boy; black curls an' blue eyes an' she called 'im "Master Tom". Right funny it was.'

Mum said nothing although she realised that the child must have been the son of the lady of the house. Granny continued.

'She sat me in a wooden chair and she made me understand that she was going upstairs for a minute.'

'How did you understand Granny?' asked my cousin Violet.

'Do you think I's a Dinlo?' Granny snapped, getting into a temper. 'She came right back with another lady. Real Gentry she was. She 'ad lovely 'air an' fingernails an' a pretty blue frock with lace on the front. Well she sits down at the table an' puts 'alf a crown in front o' me an' then she 'eld out 'er 'and t' me. I knowed what she wanted. I knowed she was well off so I touched 'er bit o' vonger an' shakes me 'ead. "No, No," I says. She was clever all right. She knowed what I meant. She puts down another 'alf crown. Now,' said Granny, leaning forward, "ere was the clever bit! I could see by the look in 'er eye that she was sad. I could see summat was missin' in 'er life. I didn't know what 'twas but that didn't make no matter. She 'eld out 'er 'and an' she gazed into me eyes so pleadin' like, I knowed of a sudden what t' say. "My dear," I said, "'Ee's bin so sad but within a year everythin' will be good fer 'ee with much joy!" I thought t' meself, that gives me plenty o' scope! The lady took me 'and, an' the tears just rained down 'er cheeks. I put the five shillin' in me purse. The little boy came an' stood by me and smiled an' the lady asked me if I 'ad many grandchildren. Well, I think she did. I said "Yes, many!"'

Granny laughed and held up her basket full of beautiful baby clothes. At the time my brother Nelson was the youngest, being about eighteen months old. Granny told us that the lady had spoken to the young woman who had returned with the large bundle of baby clothes. The lady had given it to Granny and to her amazement she had embraced Granny and kissed her on both cheeks. As Granny recounted it she still looked dazed. It is not often that a Gypsy is kissed by a lady and Granny was not a woman who appreciated being hugged or kissed – especially by strangers. The little boy baby clothes all had a French label. Mum could not believe her eyes. There was everything a child could need; little embroidered dungarees, playsuits, little hand-smocked shirts, even little socks and shoes in various sizes.

'Take 'em Mary. No need to tell anybuddy else.'

Mum did not argue. She was only too pleased not to have to worry about dressing my little brother. Even Teddy, my next brother, wore some of those lovely clothes as well because Mum washed everything so carefully and the quality was so good. That is why people stared when Mum took them out in their lovely French clothes; two little Gypsy boys dressed like princes.

We wondered what happened to the French lady. Did she ever get what she wanted? We asked Granny one day.

'Not at first,' said Granny. 'I got worried 'cause she was getting real skinny. I still called. I wanted t' see if me words would come true. She allus looked the picture o' misery when I did see 'er. She met me at the gate a short while back with more hugs and kisses. I knowed summat was all right. She sat me down in 'er kitchen, put a saucepan o' milk on t' boil. I thought, what's goin' on? Then she put cocoa powder an' sugar into the milk an' poured it into two tall glasses in little silver 'olders with two fluffy sweets on top and grated chocolate over the lot. Well!' Granny stopped and shook her head in wonder. 'She put some little biscuits on the plate and puts it in front o' me. "Drink! Drink!" she says. Honest to God, I've never tasted a drink like it in my life! She saw my look. "Good! Good!" she says, "Hot chocolate!" Then she showed me a baby's jacket she bin knittin' and she patted 'er tummy. "Bebe – me bebe!" she says. What a relief! Summat turned out right after all!'

'What did she have Granny?' we asked.

'A little gal child,' said Granny. I did see 'er fer about a year or so after but then they went off back to France. The last time I seen 'er she 'ugged me and kissed me again! That's the way they do things in France.'

Granny looked quite disgruntled.

'I 'opes it don't catch on yer!'

How things go full circle. It is only on looking back that we see the whole picture. My children had nearly all grown up by now. Sarah was married with a baby son, James, so I was now a grandmother. Virginia was working in the town and soon to be married. Claire and Daniel had just started senior school and were doing well. The house was full on Saturday afternoons when they all came to visit, not to mention other family members who would drop in for a cuppa. Life was full and busy at home as well as at work.

I met Mrs Ashley on a bright spring morning at the end of February. She was in her large garden surrounded by hundreds of daffodils. At once I recalled standing up in class and reciting one of my favourite poems, 'Daffodils' by William Wordsworth. The picture it evokes in my mind of a beautiful girl lying on a couch while hundreds of daffodils swayed in the warm breeze is delightful. Mrs Ashley was small and stout with her hair in a large bun. Little curly tendrils were blowing around her face. She gave me a warm smile and her face was full of dimples. I liked her at once.

'Come in,' she said. 'Let's have a hot drink.'

We went into her spacious kitchen and I explained that I would be coming for two hours a week to start with.

'That's fine at the moment,' she nodded, 'I only need you to vacuum through and if you can manage to move the smaller pieces of furniture, I will be pleased with that.'

There was hardly anything else that needed doing. Her home was very elegant and well kept. After an hour she insisted that I sit down.

'Come along, I have a few things I want you to know about me and my family,' she said. 'If you would like to tell me a bit about yourself, that would be very nice. Go and sit in the lounge and I will make the coffee today. In future, you can do it.'

Family group. John, me, Sarah, Virginia, Daniel and
Claire visiting Mum at the camp

Sarah and Virginia spending a week with Mum.
They loved being together – always smiling

A day at the beach for Sarah and Virginia –
happy together

A lovely day out, stopping for a picnic. John took the photo

My dear father with a small friend.
Mum always cut bits off photos

Sarah, Daniel, Claire and Virginia (seated) in our garden.
Happy in each other's company

At home on our silver wedding anniversary

On our golden wedding anniversary. Where have the years gone?

John with one of the working steam engines
he built himself

Her living room was very comfortable. It was full of books and pictures and here and there were huge bowls of daffodils. How lovely, I thought, sitting down in a comfy armchair. The door opened and she came in with coffee and biscuits.

'I feel guilty sitting here with you waiting on me,' I said to her.

'This is your first day,' she smiled. 'Make the most of it!'

She told me a little of her life, past and present, as we sipped our coffee. It was all very interesting. She had three daughters and one son. She saw two of her daughters and son often but she made no mention of the youngest. I did not ask. I knew from experience that there was probably some upset that she could not mention just yet. I told her that I too had four children, three daughters and one son.

'Sarah and Virginia, Daniel and Claire. Daniel and Claire are the youngest – twins!'

'Oh, how lovely!' she smiled.

'My eldest daughter was a nursemaid to a cousin of Prince Charles!' she said, proudly. Her other daughter and son were in business. She paused and looked me in the eye.

'My youngest daughter is ... quite mad. She's being taken care of by a family trained to do it. I just couldn't cope with her.'

'That's very sad,' I said. 'Is she happy where she is?'

'I hope so. The trouble is she often slips away and tries to find me. I love her, but she is so difficult. She's never harmed anyone and I don't think she ever would but

I've lost many of my private helpers because they were frightened of her. Social Services have been more than kind. And here you are! I do hope you stay.' She looked sad and pleading. At that moment I could have promised anything but I kept quiet and just smiled. Truth to tell, I was a bit nervous but I reasoned to myself that I would probably never see her. Mrs Ashley went into the garden while I washed the coffee things. She returned with her arms full of daffodils. Wrapping them in tissue paper, she placed them in my arms. I was overcome. I would never pick my own flowers from the garden, I often bought them instead. I was like my father in that respect who said he preferred to see the flowers growing outside.

'How kind of you!' I said.

'I could see by your eyes how much you admired my daffodils and I have so many that I won't even notice that they've been picked.'

After that she always gave me flowers from her garden in their season.

Some weeks later I was alone in her kitchen, turning out her cupboards. I was kneeling down. As I went to stand, I felt a hand on my head, pressing me down very firmly. To say my blood ran cold is an understatement. I began to shake and my throat was so dry that I had no voice.

'Stay. Stay,' said a voice, then very loudly, 'Mother! Mother!'

Oh yes, I knew who it was now so I stayed where I was. The kitchen door crashed open.

'Mother, I have caught a thief red-handed!' said the

voice. I nearly had a fit of nervous giggles but I managed to restrain myself and kept calm. Mrs Ashley's voice was gentle.

'All right Eliza. That is very clever of you, but this kind lady is helping me sort out my cupboards.'

'Oh!' said Eliza in a disappointed tone. 'I did so want to help you mother.'

'Let her stand up Eliza and then you can see for yourself,' Mrs Ashley said firmly, but in a tone that showed the strain she was under. I tried to stand. Eliza promptly gave me a helping hand, placing her arms around my waist and giving me a hefty tug. When I was in a standing position, I realised that my eyes were tightly closed.

'Is she dead?' Eliza asked in a very interested manner.

'No, no. I'm all right!' I gasped, opening my eyes. In front of me stood a beautiful young woman with bright blue eyes, a mass of black curls and a set of pretty white teeth. I smiled back and quickly sat down. Mrs Ashley had gone to phone someone and explained what had happened. She was arranging to have Eliza collected. When she returned she looked worn out and sat in another chair. Meanwhile, Eliza created havoc. No cupboard was left unopened and no food was left untasted, except the frozen food, which she started to throw in the bin.

'This is too hard! No one can eat it!' she grumbled. Suddenly she stopped and made a beeline for me. I braced myself, not knowing what to expect. Putting her mouth to my ear she began to whisper. At first it was unintelligible, just whispering. Then I nearly fell off my chair. This angelic-looking young woman was filling my ears with the most pornographic filth I hope I will never have to experience again. I guessed that this was part of her illness. I turned and gently tried to remove her clinging fingers but it was no good. She became more agitated. Mrs Ashley was in tears. I felt deeply sorry for her. I managed to distract her by offering her a sweet and eventually some people arrived and gently persuaded her into a car, which drove away. Her mother turned to me, in tears.

'Forgive me my dear. I shouldn't have exposed you to this.'

'Sit down,' I comforted, 'I don't have to be home early. I'll stay and get this kitchen sorted.'

She watched me in silent gratitude while I tried to restore order from chaos. I thought how hard it must be to live with the worries she had. Just as I was leaving, her eldest daughter came up the drive. She put her arms around her mother in sympathy. Mrs Ashley's daughter insisted on driving me home.

'You must be worn out,' she said.

'I'm more concerned about your mum.'

'We've had to put up with this since Eliza was born. Don't get me wrong. We all adore Eliza. It's not her fault.' Her eldest daughter went on to tell me that she herself had never married. 'Life got in the way of living. I've had a wonderful life though. I've travelled the world and met people of all nationalities and religions. I've mothered dozens of children whose own parents were too busy with their own lives to spend the time with them.'

She was nursemaid at that time to a lord and lady's children. I told her that my eldest daughter was married and had an eighteen-month-old son, James: our first adored grandchild. I did not mind being called 'Granny'. I was very proud and still young enough to enjoy it, being forty-one when he was born.

'I've got some very nice clothes that will fit your little James,' she said. 'They were kept for best and hardly worn. The children are grown out of them now.'

'Thank you. I'm sure Sarah will be glad of them,' I said, and thought no more about it.

A few weeks later, Mrs Ashley handed me a large bag of baby things. I looked through them with delight. There were a set of navy blue velvet pantaloons and sailor top with knee-length socks to match, little shirts and dungarees, little shoes and socks – all as good as new. They looked very expensive with labels in French. At once I remembered Granny and the beautiful baby clothes that the French lady had given her many years ago and how my little brothers had looked like princes when my mother took them out. With the clothes were some very nice white baby towels and a hairbrush.

I stayed with Mrs Ashley for several years until she moved to Ireland. I met her eldest daughter again sometime later and she told me that Eliza had died. How, she did not say. The problems they had had with her were now alleviated but they missed her very much.

'Just looking at her beautiful face somehow made it all worthwhile,' she told me. 'We did love her. I hope she knew that.'

They had obviously loved her. For many years they had cared for her at home and spent nearly every penny trying to get Eliza the right treatment. As they all grew older they no longer had the strength or the resources to do everything for her. They had nothing to reproach themselves for. Nothing at all.

18

Broom

My mother had come on one of her weekly visits. It was a lovely day and we sat in the garden enjoying a cup of tea. I suddenly noticed how tired she looked. She never complained or said she felt a bit poorly, even though she had had a serious illness fifteen years before and had nearly died then. She was only in her late sixties but I began to feel concerned.

'Mum, if we could get you into a little bungalow with a garden a bit nearer us, would you take it?'

'I don't know, Rosie,' she said. 'Aunt Betsy would miss me. We help each other.'

'Think about it Mum. It's up to you.'

Meanwhile, I applied to the council. A few weeks later Mum was offered a flat. I did not even tell her. No, I thought, Mum must have her own front door and a garden. She would never worry about the lack of any modern conveniences because she had always managed without them, but a garden that she could step out of her own front door into was so important to her. Shortly after she was offered the tenancy of a one-bedroom bungalow. We took her to see it and she fell in love with it straight away.

'Oh look, Rosie. It's got a garden!'

I was so glad. It was just big enough for Mum to plant her own things and very quiet and private. It was just ten minutes walk away from us. Mum had to tell Aunt Betsy and Aunt Britt she would be leaving the camp but she was not looking forward to it. They were both very upset when she did but I explained that we needed to have Mum living nearer to me.

'She won't be 'appy!' Aunt Betsy grumbled. 'She's used to we lot. We'll miss 'er.'

'I know,' I said, 'but she's not that far away. She can still come and visit you.'

'It won't be the same.' Aunt Betsy did her best to try and persuade Mum to stay. I knew that my mother was torn but we never tried to persuade her or expect her to do what we wanted. Mum had a quiet will of her own.

The day she left her little blue caravan, she went around her garden taking slips and cuttings.

'I'll just push this in and it'll soon grow,' she said.

She stood for some while looking into the distance, remembering, as she told me later, Sam the pig who we children played with after school and her little bantam chicks. She would save their eggs for the little ones' tea. They always felt special when they were given two tiny eggs in tiny egg cups. The raspberry canes and strawberry beds were prolific and we almost became bored with strawberries and raspberries for tea. She thought of Tiny, my dog, who waited for me at the bottom of the wagon steps. Mum fell over her daily but put up with her because she loved me so much. The visits of the travelling Gypsies, Nellie and her kilt, Granny and Granfer who had given us all a home and space to grow; so many memories overwhelmed her.

But move she did and she and her new garden flourished. Shortly before she died, she told my brother Ted that she had spent the happiest years of her life in her little bungalow. Mum had been brought up in a large house as a child so she soon felt at home in the bungalow, turning it into a little palace full of photos of her family. We had a phone installed for her, which pleased her no end, and she spent many happy hours ringing everyone up.

'I'm only at the end of the phone!' She would say.

Yes, she was.

One particular Monday morning I was sent to a lady of eighty-three. She lived at the time in a third-floor flat and appeared to be fit and well, despite the steps. The three flights of stairs did not bother me but as I went up them I did wonder how she coped. She had left the door open for me so I walked straight in, calling out a greeting as I did so. A little dumpling of a lady came to meet me; very clean and tidy with white curly hair and rosy cheeks.

'Come in, my dear. Let's have a cup of tea and get to know each other a little bit,' she said.

She quickly made the tea and we sat down. For the next fifteen or twenty minutes she never stopped talking. She learned nothing about me except my name and that I would be coming once a week to start with and then twice a week when there was a space available. She not only talked nineteen to the dozen but did so while drinking her tea and eating two huge home-made buttered scones. She offered one to me but, although they looked very nice, I think I would have choked. She ate both scones in about two or three minutes, talking all the while and spitting crumbs with every word. She never changed her habits all the while I was her home help.

I found Annie to be very strange with her fixed ideas but also very interesting. She followed me around while I was working, talking all the time except when I was using the vacuum cleaner. She would often tell me the same story over and over.

'When I was a girl, I was the eldest of nine, my father worked for a very poor wage and my dear mother worked from morning 'til night, making our clothes, working in the garden, cleaning and cooking. She was a shadow of the lovely girl my father had wed. We all loved our dear Mam but she had no time for us all. The day I was thirteen, my father (we called him "Pa") told me that he'd found me a job at the local Manse. I was to live in for five shillings a week. I would be cooking and cleaning under the housekeeper. She would expect me to work from six in the morning 'til after supper (the time of which might vary). I had one day off a week and I had to send half of my wages home. My Pa said he would come and collect it himself so I was left with half a crown to last the week. Still, I thought, I would have nothing to spend my money on so I will save it up and one day I will find a place of my own.'

At this point she stopped to draw breath, so I managed to interject.

'You have a very cosy flat.' It was. Red velvet curtains and floral loose covers matched a red hearth rug. A Christmas cactus in a copper bowl stood on a table, also with red flowers hanging over the edge. There was a lot of red but the whole room looked cheerful, bright and clean. She saw me admiring it.

'This is the room I've always wanted,' she said. 'I've worked hard all my life. I married happily when I was in my late forties but my husband died five years ago. I miss him very much. I've only one friend and a few relatives I see regularly, but I don't need people.'

She came across as very hard. I soon learned that her life had made her so.

'How did you get on in your first job?' I asked. For a brief moment I could see the woman she had been.

'They treated me like a skivvy!' she spat, 'I scrubbed and cleaned and I washed and scrubbed some more, then I cooked and washed up. I was just thirteen; just a little girl but they made no allowance for my age. One day my hands got so red raw, I couldn't do my work. They took me to their doctor, a very kind man, and told him to give me something for my hands. He told them that my hands would have to heal before I could put them in water again. All the Missus could say was "who's going to do the washing?"' Annie smiled as she relished the memory of the doctor's rage.

' "Here we have a child!" he said. "You are not taking care of her. If you make any attempt to make her work before her hands are healed, I will make sure your parishioners know all about it!" And with that he showed her out. So, they had no choice. They had to allow my hands to heal properly. I hated every minute I spent working for them. I was saving all of my money so that I could leave and find another job. I had been there about ten months and I had saved five pounds, a huge amount of money to me. I had hidden it at the back of a drawer in my bedroom. Beside it, wrapped in an old nightie, I had a silver-backed brush, mirror and comb set. My Ma had given it to me the day I left home. I would never part with it. Her mistress, who she had worked for before she was married to Pa, had given it to her as a wedding gift. Anyway, this particular day, I was sent out on an errand. I liked doing that as it got me out of the house, although the basket was very heavy on the way home. I arrived home about an hour later and was called into the minister's office. When I entered the room, I saw him, his wife, his sister and the housekeeper all standing there and on the desk was a pile of half-crowns and my Ma's brush and mirror set.'

Annie stopped to draw a breath and strengthen her posture. Then she continued.

'I was *boiling* with rage! I stepped forward with the intention of taking back my belongings but his sister grabbed my arm and pulled me away. "What are you doing with my private belongings?" I shouted. "Give them back!" Then the minister spoke. "What I want to know," he says, "is whose belongings they *really* are. Not yours obviously!" Suddenly, I was quite calm. "They are all mine. My mother gave me the gift that her mistress (a real lady) gave her on her wedding day. The money is what I've saved from what I have earned here, so that I can leave your employment, which I have hated ever since I started!" They said I was an ungrateful girl and they had done their best for me since I had been there. I said, "And I've done my best to please you, but you don't want to be pleased, you only want to be cruel!" Then I collected up my possessions, turned my back and left the room. I went straight upstairs and put my few things in a bag and without even combing my hair, I walked out!'

'What?' I teased her. 'You never even combed your hair?'

She smiled at that. Annie was very proud of her white hair.

'My hair was brown then,' she laughed, 'but I just wanted to leave. "Stop!" he called after me. I just ignored him and walked down the path and through the gate and turned around to look at them all. I wanted to make a point. There they were, all staring at me with open mouths; the big window framed them perfectly. Staring right back at them, I lifted each foot in turn and ostentatiously shook the dust off my shoes. He's a minister, I thought. He knows what that means!'

I nodded and smiled. I knew what it meant too.

'I walked off down the road and then, suddenly, the tears came. What was I going to do? I sat on a bench under a nearby tree. I read the inscription: "Our love to Daddy who loved this place." Then all of a sudden, I felt a kind hand touch my arm and I heard a voice say, "What's the matter, child?"'

'Who was it?' I asked.

'It was the doctor who had treated my hands months before. I told him the whole story. When I got to the bit about shaking the dust off my shoes, I thought he would never stop laughing. "I'll make quite sure that they don't get away with this," he said. "Meanwhile, this is my lucky day! My wife needs some help in the house, maybe you could give us a try?" I was overjoyed! "Oh yes," I said, "I would love to give you a try!" That "try" lasted until the day I got married. Those lovely people made my life worthwhile.'

'I'm glad you were strong enough to make a stand. There are many people as young as you were who would not be able to stand up for themselves as you did.'

Then I made the mistake of giving my own opinion.

'Even though you thought you were alone, God had his eyes upon you and you ended up with very kind employers who took the place of your parents until you were able to help yourself.'

To my amazement she turned on me.

'Oh, no! I will never believe anything like that! It's just a fairy story! I've never relied on anyone but me and sometimes my husband.'

'So,' I said gently, 'you think it's just a coincidence that the doctor turned up and gave you a home and a job and showed you lots of love?'

She said no more but she looked thoughtful and I got on with my work. I got to thinking, though, that many people make judgements about God by the behaviour of those who claim to represent Him but I never mentioned the subject with her again.

I got on very well with Annie and I admired her very much. She was well into her eighties but she cooked her own meals and baked cakes, knitted and sewed all her own clothes. I began to realise that the doctor and his wife had had a bargain. She told me she had done all of this and more for the doctor and his wife and was glad to do it.

She could be very hard at times. What Annie believed or did not believe was cut in stone. I only saw her in tears once, when her friend died. I arrived one morning to find her, just as usual, bright as a button. I knew how fond Annie was of her friend. Hardly a day would pass without them sharing a pot of tea. I had heard from a colleague that her friend had died. I said nothing at first. I wanted to see if she wished to talk about it or not. After a while I noticed her staring at the teapot and wringing at a tea towel. Without saying a word, I just put my arms around her and patted her back. The tears flowed, hers and mine. She sobbed brokenheartedly.

'What will I do without her? She was so kind and very gentle.'

'You were very blessed to have such a good friend for so many years. You will miss her. You will have many good times to remember, though, and in time the pain of parting will ease,' I said softly. I thought it a shame she would take no more comfort than that. I stayed with Annie until she was in her nineties when she started to forget things and behave strangely. She went into a nursing home like many of my other ladies and I went to see her a few times, but out of the context of her own home she did not know me. She seemed happy enough in her new little world and I have always remembered her.

My father taught me that God created us and every good thing was provided by Him and his son, Jesus Christ. I accepted this completely and I still do. This was the limit of his teaching but it was a very good start. I remember a work colleague telling me she was an atheist and that anyone who believed in a Creator or Jesus was really strange. At the same time, she was buying Christmas gifts for people she hardly knew. When I pointed out that her behaviour was stranger than mine, she nearly choked.

'Well, you are supposed to be celebrating the birthday of someone you don't even believe in. How strange is that?'

She did not know how to answer me and the matter was closed. All of my Gypsy family believed in a Creator, although none of them went to church except for weddings and funerals. Gypsies back then rarely christened their children. Times may have changed. They are brought up as mine were, with a strong faith, but they must make their own decision when they are old enough. My father had never set foot in a church, neither had any of us children, but we all knew who to thank for all the good things we enjoyed daily from the beauty of the fields, trees and sky to the food we had on our plates that grew fresh from the earth. Yet my father had a very strong faith in God. He knew that nothing would grow or be harvested without the good

Lord's help and he enjoyed everything in its season. I will always remember watching my father as he stood in the blossoming bean field. His head was flung back and his eyes closed as he breathed in the perfume of the bean blossoms.

'Rosie,' he had said to me, 'it's a smell like no other, and all free!'

I had always taken it for granted, but since then I make a point of stopping our car whenever we pass a blossoming bean field in order to enjoy that wonderful smell – all free.

We had strong evidence all around us in our daily lives that there was a God and I personally have had my prayers answered. The wonders of nature, the times and the seasons which we calmly expected to arrive on time, the thousands of wild flowers that bloomed in the fields around us and the fish in the river we played in all testified to a Great Designer. We never took such beauty for granted. These things cost nothing and my mother always had a posy of wild flowers on a shelf, freshly picked each day by her children.

I found it difficult to understand how any father could expect his thirteen-year-old daughter to be a skivvy to complete strangers and then wash his hands of her except for the weekly half-crown. Gypsy parents would never have done this, no matter how tough times were. They look after their families, old or young. They always made sure there was an extra dinner in the pot, just in case there was someone who needed it. My own mother was often ill when I was a child yet she never had to worry that we children would be left hungry.

Sometimes I would make a comment on the food I was given. I would say:

'Mammy doesn't cook her carrots like this,' or 'Mammy don't burn her roast taters!' only to be told, 'Be quiet Rosie and be glad yer got a dinner!'

I was glad of it when I later realised how short they must have been themselves. But nothing was begrudged. Granfer was my hero. Many was the time he pressed a coin into my hand and said, 'Yer me pretty. 'Ee give this t' yer Mammy. Say nothing t' nobuddy!'

My aunties made sure we were clean and dressed if Mum was ill but I would let no one except my mother touch my hair. When she had been ill almost a week they tried to round me up to brush it.

'Come yer baby Rosie! Yer looks like yer bin pulled through a 'edge backwards!'

'No!' I screamed, 'I wants Mammy to brush it!' and off I ran, straight into Uncle Alfie's waiting hand.

'Look at yer, yer bad gal. Yer looks like a dirty tramp!' he scolded. Then, tugging me into the wash-house, he took down the horse brush and a length of raffia. Ignoring my screams of rage, he brushed my hair until my scalp tingled. By now there were quite a few onlookers.

'That's right, Alfie,' said Granny. 'She be lookin' a right mess!'

Granfer disagreed and I looked up hopefully.

'Ah, let the poor little gal be, Alfie!'

'No. I be fed up with lookin' at 'er. It's enough t' put yer off yer grub seein' that furze bush she got on 'er 'ead! I dunno what 'er father be thinkin' of. 'E won't do it 'cause she cries. Well, she can cry! The more she cries the longer it'll take!'

Even I could see the wisdom in this, so I stopped yelling. Uncle Alfie carried on brushing my hair back so tight, I thought my nose would end up on my forehead. He finished it with one long plait and tied it with the raffia. I cannot remember looking in a mirror but my mother remarked how tidy it was a week later when she was better and finally able to do it herself.

'Look at your hair, it's a mass of curls!' said Mum, brushing it out.

'Yes,' I said, idly leaning against her knee, 'but I likes *you* doing my hair Mammy!'

The warm, friendly family community that I experienced as a child was a far cry from the treatment I have witnessed or heard of over many years.

19

Queen of the Meadows

Mrs Harper was in her mid-sixties and spoke with a posh but pretty voice. When I knew her a little better I commented on it, saying you could tell a lot about a person from their voice. She agreed.

'With you, though, it's not your voice I noticed, but the way you speak. I have heard that way many times before but I will say no more just yet,' she smiled. She said this in such a pleasant way that I was content to leave things as they were.

She lived in a pretty flat, which overlooked fields and a river at the back. Sometimes there were cows and horses wandering through the field and in the spring and summer it was full of wild flowers.

'You have a lovely view,' I said.

'I know. I enjoy every moment, sitting here having my meals.'

She was a little reserved and some of her ways were a bit odd. She gave me what she called a 'hot drink' when

I was longing for a cup of tea but I was given a glass of warm water with a fizzing tablet in it.

'Oh!' I said in surprise. 'What's this?'

'It will do you good,' she said sharply.

'I'm sorry, but I don't drink or eat anything unless I know what it is first.'

'It's only a vitamin C tablet.'

'Do I look as though I need one then?' I asked, putting it on the draining board. She shook her head.

'No, you look very well. But I enjoy a vitamin drink myself, so I thought you might.'

'I've had many drinks offered to me in my job,' I said. 'The worst was twice-used tea bags!'

'What?' she gasped.

'Yes, so I'm very careful now.'

She put the kettle on at once and made a lovely fresh cup of tea.

'Almost as good as my Granfer's!' I teased.

'Is that a compliment?'

'If you had ever met my Granfer you would know it was the best.'

I stood up and washed the cups and saucers. No mugs for her. I liked to get to know my clients a bit first so I did not want to tell her too much just yet. Gradually she opened up to me. She was a woman after my own heart. She was really clean over the things that mattered and clean over things that were not so important. We got along very well and she began to tell me a little about her life. Her family were not rich but they had run a village shop and had sent her to a private school where her life had been a misery but where she had been taught to speak well. This had certainly been a benefit to her. When her parents had died she sold the shop and put the money in the bank. Then she made a huge mistake and married a tall, dark, handsome man who managed to get through her money in a very short time. I was saddened to hear that she had been taken advantage of.

'It was my own fault,' she said. 'I packed my bags and took all I had left of my jewellery and waited until he was out. Then I ran a long, long way away. I've never seen him since. I don't know if he's dead or alive and I don't care. Anyway, soon it won't matter.'

'It seems a shame you didn't have a child,' I said.

'Oh but I did! I have a son. I didn't know any better but I was pregnant when I left.'

'So where is your son now?'

'He's married to someone out of the top drawer. That's what she thinks and what he wants me to think. She only mixes with the upper classes. I rarely see them and they certainly don't want to see me.'

She looked at me with a twinkle in her eye.

'I regret to say that she would not wish to mix with *you*, my dear,' she said, then looking into my face she added, 'but that would be *her* loss.'

Well, I thought, she knows her own mind. Shortly afterwards she went into a private hospital paid for by her son. He also kept his eye on her flat for two or three weeks. When she came home I resumed my visits. When I first saw her I could tell that she had been very ill. She was in tears when she showed me the damage that had been done to her antique dining table. It had been a valuable piece. She has shown me the offer she had been made for it a few months before. I did not like it, personally. It had a strange surface and looked as though a darker polish had been rubbed in the grooves. Apparently, neither did her daughter-in-law as she had taken wire wool to it and had scrubbed as hard as she could, trying to remove the polish. She had ruined it completely. It would cost hundreds of pounds to restore. Her daughter-in-law could not understand what she had done wrong and had stormed out in a rage.

'I don't want her false airs and graces here any more,' she said, 'and I don't suppose I will see my son from now on. I know how spiteful she can be.'

Oh dear, I thought. I made her a cup of tea and put some of my own chocolate biscuits on a tray in front of her fire. She sat down in the winged chair with a sigh of relief. I covered her up with a rug and sat opposite her.

'Oh if only I had known what my life was going to end up like.'

'It's just as well we don't,' I said. She looked at me sideways.

'Do you think I don't know about *you*?' she twinkled.

'I would be very surprised if you knew all about me,' I replied carefully. 'You may have guessed correctly something about me but whatever you think you know you will almost certainly be wrong.'

I was not quite sure what she meant but I had an idea.

'Stop, stop!' she said and went on to explain. 'When I left my husband I was very scared. I rented a cottage at the bottom of a lane. I was very lonely. One day, the Gypsies and their wagons and horses arrived. I was even more scared. I was young and pregnant and alone. I did have some money. I made sure my husband did not have it all. I knew absolutely nothing about the Romanies. They didn't bother me at all and I became curious to say the least. One day I went up to the camp to say "hello" and I was fascinated.'

I was watching her carefully to see where she was going with this.

'To cut a long story short, I almost became one of them. We became good friends. The women were absolutely beautiful and the children so cared for. I had my son when I lived there and they helped me out a lot. He played with the Gypsy children every day. When my son was four I moved to a town. It was for the best. It seems so snobbish now, but I didn't want other children's parents to stop their children playing with him because he was friends with them. Now I think how much nicer he might have turned out if we had stayed where we were.'

'You don't know that for sure,' I said. 'There's good and bad everywhere.'

'I just don't know where I've gone wrong,' she whimpered. She looked up at me.

'As soon as I saw you, I *knew* there was something different about you. There's something in the way you speak. I can't even tell you what it is, but I recognised it immediately.'

There was a mutual knowledge between us that went unspoken for now but we left it there. I had things to do. I became very fond of Mrs Harper. I began to notice little things about her. She was losing weight and losing interest in things that she had enjoyed. I was concerned.

Later on, after I had done some shopping I went to see if she was all right. Her door was unlatched. I went in and called her name softly.

'Come in, Rosie. I'm in here!' she called back. She was sitting in a cold room in her dressing gown. She looked pitiful.

'Oh, Rosie, I was on my own. I don't have anybody,' she wept. I sat down and clasped her poor cold hands in mine.

'Yes you have. I'm here.'

I looked into her eyes. She was terminally ill and would need more help than I could give her. I rang the office and they arranged for her to go back into hospital. Then I built her a fire, made her a bowl of soup and brought her a bowl of warm water and soap so I could help her get ready for the ambulance. I got her lipstick and powder and after she was made up she said she felt much better.

'Now,' I explained gently, 'I think you will have to go back into the hospital because you are very poorly. I know you don't want me to call your son, but please let me this time.'

She nodded silently. I got through to the daughter-in-law who was quite frosty at first. I spoke to her as kindly as I could and she said that they would be there within the hour. I waited to see her off in the ambulance. I kissed her cheek and she touched my hand.

'Rosie, I've always liked you. You're a good girl.'

'That's what my mother used to say,' I replied.

I left a note for her son. She died within a week. I thought it was such a tragedy to be left alone, ill and neglected, to die and no one knows or even wonders why they have not seen you for weeks; such a contrast with the Romany way of life. I wondered how many millions the Gypsy way must have been saving on care home bills.

My mother told me some of her neighbours were being moved out of their home when I visited soon after.

'Look,' she pointed. 'They've been there for years. It can't be right.'

'No,' I sighed, 'but if they have no family, it must be difficult.'

'I hope that I never have to go into a home,' said Mum, looking me in the eye.

'Mum, as long as I'm alive, you'll never have to.'

What I remember most about this conversation is that when I gave my mother this assurance, Mum accepted it completely. She never mentioned it again. My mother only lived in her bungalow for six years before she died in her seventies. She loved her little home and garden and we all visited her regularly. The week before she died, we had all been to see her. Sarah commented that we had no idea that she would die but were all glad we had seen her that week.

The last time I saw my mother was the afternoon before she died. It was a lovely October day and the roses still tumbled over the garden walls. Their perfume still hung in the air.

'Oh, what a wonderful day it's been. Especially for October.'

She turned to me, took my hand and said, 'you've always been there for me Rosie.'

'I've tried to be,' I said.

Mum was always there for us. She died the next morning, sitting in her armchair, reading the paper. It was completely unexpected. The doctor asked how I had known so quickly. I told him my mother had not turned up to meet me as promised. Mum would never have let me down so I knew immediately that something had happened to her.

My mother had lived for twenty-five years after Dad. She coped very well and she never needed to ask for help, especially not from Social Services. Sarah took my mother's funeral service as Mum had told us years before she died that she did not want a clergyman who did not even know her taking the service. I can still see Sarah's eyes, full of tears, as she stood there. She spoke about the happy times they had had on holiday together, of the way my mother never let you go home empty-handed. The organist played 'I'll take you home again Kathleen', which Dad used to sing to her, as Kathleen was her given name although she had always been called Mary. Afterwards many people said to me that they would like to be so blessed when their time came. The funeral director told me that it was one of the most beautiful services that he had ever heard. 'Your mother would have loved it,' he said. My young nephew said the same. I know for sure she would have. Sarah was her adored first grandchild and spent many hours with her Granny.

Mum had her wish. She never went into a home. She had died quickly and quietly in her own home. I found her camera after the funeral. She had taken photos of the babies in the family. Mum never took a good photo. They were always on the slant or, because she was so short, the heads were cut off, but these were the best I had ever known her to take. One that Sarah had taken of her was the last shot. She was smiling while holding her latest grandchild, Danny, who was four and a half months, in her arms. I missed her then and I miss her still.

The week after her funeral I rang her number, almost hoping I would hear her chirpy voice at the other end saying, 'Hello, Rosie, hello!' But I was never to hear her again. We all miss her still but my memories are very clear. Whenever I think of her, she is standing in a flowerbed or picking her fruit from her Cox's Orange Pippin tree, happy as a queen.

20

Wild Iris

Walking to work one beautiful sunny morning, I found myself wishing that I had the day off. There was a tang of autumn in the air. Apples and pears were hanging heavily on the trees. I could see apples on the pavements and lying on the grass in the gardens and I could smell the sweet scent of rotten fruit. My goodness, I thought, what a waste! My Granny and mother would have been in seventh heaven with all this bounty. Still, times had changed. The shops were all full of food, most of it quite cheap. There was no need for anyone to go without.

Olivia Ann and Beatrice May were two elderly sisters who lived together in a pretty cottage in the village. Beatrice May was a widow with no children and Olivia Ann was tall and slim and suffered from Alzheimer's. Beatrice May ran the house with a little help from me four hours a week. That was the time they were allotted but they were so tidy the work was minimal. They were both charming ladies and I liked them very much, although I felt patronised some of the time. It was the way Beatrice May spoke down to me. If a friend of theirs called she would always introduce me by patting my arm and saying, 'This is our help, Rosemary. Isn't she *lovely*?' I know she meant well, but it made me feel about five years old. When they had something to celebrate, they would lay a little table in front of the fire with glasses of sherry and little biscuits and there we would sit; two old ladies nearly a century old and me, the help, in 'me pinny', feeling the oldest of all of us. They had beautiful manners and I did my best to keep up. Unfortunately I had a habit of crooking the little finger of my right hand, which looked a little pretentious, although I had done this since I was a child, merely to protect my finger from being burned on the hot cup. I also did this when I was having a cold drink. The two ladies gently mocked me and said I had 'delusions of grandeur'. If they had only known that they were sitting with a Gypsy girl. They probably would not have been remotely bothered. Beatrice May had worked in banking and had held a high position but she treated everyone the same and liked everyone so long as they behaved themselves at all times. Never, as Olivia Ann was wont to say, 'behaving badly and frightening the horses'. They were generous and often gave me a bunch of lily of the valley, which bloomed profusely in their garden, but, oddly, never a fresh bunch – always a day old. I found this hard to understand myself. I would have felt that I was insulting the person I was giving the flowers to.

Beatrice May often did her shopping on the days I came. She hated leaving her sister alone. This was also very wise, as Olivia Ann would wander around the house turning out drawers and cupboards or going out into the garden and asking passers-by to open jars and bottles for her. This they did, receiving a smiling 'thank you', that is, if she had not lost her false teeth again. She also loved answering the phone. Sometimes she would allow me to take it from her, at other times it would get a bit undignified as we wrestled on the sofa. The trouble was, she did not know or care who was ringing and her closing words were always the same.

'You can like it or lump it!'

I used to record the time of the call so that Beatrice May could apologise to the caller. It was always laughed off but Beatrice did find it a bit wearing at times. Olivia Ann liked to think she was a good hostess, so after Beatrice May went shopping she would ring up various friends and invite them to lunch or other meals. Everyone knew what was going on and treated her kindly. As for me, wherever I was in the house, she would call me at the top of her voice.

'Rosemary! Have you had your coffee yet?'

'Not yet, thank you. It's a bit early,' I would reply. This would go on all morning until I finally gave in and made us both a coffee, during which we would chat at cross purposes. She would tell me the most amazing fibs, which I pretended to believe. I put on shocked faces and plenty of 'oohs' and 'aahs' at the appropriate moments, which pleased her no end. When I resumed my duties she still kept asking me, 'Rosemary, have you had your coffee?' 'Yes, thank you,' I would reply for the next half hour or so. I was always thankful when Beatrice May arrived home with lots of little goodies to tempt Olivia Ann's appetite.

Olivia Ann was tall and slender. She had married a wealthy man and her life had been full of parties, cruises and wonderful clothes. Although her husband had died more than thirty years before, she still believed he was just working or away on business. Every morning, Beatrice May would dress her in her very best clothes with her daytime jewellery adorning her hands and ears and beautiful pearls hung around her neck. This made a lot of work for Beatrice May but Olivia Ann expected it. What is more, every evening at five o'clock, Olivia Ann would call her sister imperiously from her bedroom.

'Beatrice May! Beatrice May! Kindly help me get dressed for dinner. Basil will be home in an hour and I must look my best!'

Poor Beatrice May. She was usually very tired by then and the last thing she wanted to do was help her sister get bathed and dressed for dinner. Now and again she would gently coax her sister to refrain from this little routine.

'Basil's still away dear, on business. There's no need to get dressed up when there's just the two of us is there?'

This little scene would be enacted on many occasions. I felt great pity for both of them, even more so when I realised how little they ate. Yes, the table was laid with glasses for wine and water but they would dine on tiny sandwiches and a sliver of cake or fruit. Then the table would be cleared and they were both in bed by eight-thirty. I know this because Beatrice May told me, adding sadly that it did help to pass the time.

'And we are very lucky to have each other,' she said.

What delightful ladies they were; very clean in every way and always dressed to perfection. Beatrice May told me of their childhood, which was greatly privileged. Their father was a Lord Mayor. I do not know where they lived but they had albums of photos of themselves with their parents all dressed beautifully. They talked of their homes and the wonderful places they had lived and visited. I sat with Olivia Ann and looked through the albums with her. Sometimes a photo would make her remember little scenes and she would re-enact them, to our amusement.

'We have had so many happy times,' she said to me, 'and we had a very happy childhood too.'

'That,' I agreed, 'is the best thing of all. No one could ever take those wonderful memories away from you. If you ever feel sad or a little bit lonely you can talk about these lovely times together.'

'Yes indeed,' she smiled. 'When we were girls we lived near a meadow. Sister and I were allowed to take our dollies and have a picnic there. I remember it well because a stream ran down the middle and at times it had king cups, watercress or wild irises. They were bright yellow and we called them flags but we were told not to try and pick flowers from the stream even though it was shallow. We did not disobey our parents, at least not then.'

Olivia Ann was so lucid when she was remembering the past.

'We used to stand on the bridge,' she went on, 'and we would talk to each other through the hollow piping which formed the hand rail. Then we would sit on the bank and have our picnic. How we miss those wonderful sunny days.'

'But you can still talk to each other and remember them, can't you?' I said. 'I have wonderful memories myself of running through the fields and orchards, picking fruit, and I know a meadow where all kinds of flowers grow. Sometimes I pick a posy for one or two of my ladies. They only last a day or two but they bring lots of pleasure.'

'Oh!' gasped Olivia Ann, 'I so love a posy!'

'In that case I will bring you a posy the next time I come.'

'You won't forget, will you?'

'No, I won't. God's honour.' I knew I would not but I wondered if she would.

'What does that mean?' she asked.

'When I was a child and we made a promise, we would never break it if we said "God's honour". That was a sacred promise. Unbreakable.'

'Well,' she said ruefully, 'I broke my promise to my mother. We both did. And I told a lie as well.'

'Oh? What did you do that was so bad?'

'Well, one hot day when we went for a picnic, we went straight to the stream. We were so hot, we took our shoes and stockings off and then we had our picnic. The stream was full of flowers and they smelled delightful. Shall we pick some? I said. How would Mummy know we got them from the stream? Beatrice May said best not. They would look so pretty in Mummy's vase. All right then, sister said. But we couldn't quite reach

264

them from the bank so I very carefully stepped into the water. I still couldn't reach so I stepped a bit more. My foot slipped and I fell face down in the water and Beatrice May fell on top of me, pressing me deep into the water. I couldn't breathe! At last Beatrice May got off me and pulled me out. I was soaked to the skin and so was sister. We were so scared! We both looked like scarecrows. Well, I said to Beatrice May, we're wet anyway; I'll pick a few flowers for Mummy. Then she might not be cross.'

'And was she?'

'Very. I got scared and said that Beatrice May had pushed me in. I can still see the shock on sister's face when she heard me lie. She never told on me though and I've never forgotten what I did to her and she has always been so kind to me. I expect she forgot about it long ago.'

'We all do things that we regret but you were both very young. Well, time to go home,' I said, standing up to leave.

'Don't forget!' she said,

'No, of course I won't.'

The next time I visited, I walked across the fields and picked moon daisies, Queen Anne's lace, Ragged Robin and several more. I made a very pretty posy. Olivia Ann remembered my promise as soon as she saw me walk in with her posy. You would have thought it was the most beautiful thing. I suppose it was.

'Oh! A wild flower posy! How very pretty! Look sister!'

'Yes,' said Beatrice May. Fetching a glass bowl, she sat down with her sister and arranged them.

'They don't really need to be arranged,' said Beatrice May, 'they have a natural beauty. Remember the meadow we played in when we were children?' She gazed at the flowers with a faraway look on her face.

'What fun we had, didn't we sister?'

'Oh yes,' said Olivia Ann, smiling.

Yes, I picked many wild flower posies for my ladies, but none was more appreciated than the one I picked for Beatrice May and Olivia Ann.

21

Forget–me-not

For at least a year and a half I had come to realise that the time had arrived for me to leave the Home Care service. Only that morning I had met my Waterloo. Literally. I had bent down to pick up a towel that had fallen behind the toilet and then realised that I could not get up. After a while, I managed to lever myself against the wall and then stand. I felt ridiculous. I was here to help, not put myself in a position where I was forced to ask my client if she could help *me*. Very reluctantly, I handed in my notice.

I had been working for Social Services for more years than I had originally intended. I loved the freedom that I had to use my own initiative and make my own decisions on many things and yet I still had the support from my office if I ever needed help. My supervisor and the other office staff were well trained and very good at their jobs. In the twenty-one years that I finally clocked up I had met nothing but kindness and support. I had very little to complain about.

We had regular meetings and my fellow workers were always ready to lend a hand, share a joke or give a bit of advice.

The following week I told my ladies that I would no longer be their helper but Social Services would send someone to take my place.

'Oh, but they won't be you, Rosie,' Lily said, so sadly it brought tears to my eyes.

'I'll come and visit you,' I promised each one as I hugged them goodbye. Lily had followed me to her gate, holding my hand so tightly in her arthritic one that my tears were partly because of the pain.

'Come and see me, Rosie,' she called. 'Don't be a stranger!'

I kept all my promises. I visited all of them until one by one they died or moved away. I had grown to love these strong women. I was full of admiration at their strength and decency. They had lived through two terrible wars and lost many family members yet 'we kept the flag flying,' they said, 'we kept the faith'. They certainly did. I missed them all and I still smile when I remember them.

Now I had a bit more time to think about what my life had been so far and what I might do in the future. Lying awake night after night in not a little pain, I remembered what my mother told me to do when I could not sleep. Think of happy times. So I did. I brought back all the happy memories from my childhood and recalled the long joyous days that we spent in the fields of Somerset. I picked up the little notebook that I had written anecdotes in for many years. I knew the memories would come fairly easily to me because I would never forget the wonderful years when we were all young, when day after day was spent doing the things we wanted to do, while never ever thinking they would all come to an end. When I think of my life as a Gypsy child, and later working with the elderly in their own homes, hearing their stories and seeing how they were treated by their own families, I see the people I have known as the flowers that bloom wild and free. Some remind me of those that grow stiff and straight and are then forced into designs that do not suit them at all, others prickly and unnoticed, still others delicate and sensitive – all beautiful in their own way and having their own place. All are admired by those who take the time to pick a posy for a dear friend, or others who rarely venture out of doors. I have seen the joy a posy of wild flowers brings and yet again I have seen huge bouquets of stiff shop-bought blooms, thrust without a second glance into any containers to hand and left to wither unnoticed.

I asked an elderly lady one day why she had carefully arranged a posy of wild flowers given to her by her little granddaughter in a pretty crystal bowl, placing it on a little table where she could see it, and yet put the large floral offering given to her by her son in the dining room, which was never used. At first she said the room was cooler and they would last a long time. Then with a smile she touched her posy and said, 'that little girl gave me a posy with a kiss that was full of love. He gave me his in the knowledge that I would know how expensive they were. But I think you know that my dear.'

I did know but I still felt sad that she knew too.

I grew up with nature and saw for myself what a joy it can be. How calming it is to sit and observe every wild creature doing its thing. I watched my two-year-old granddaughter, Abbie Jay, with a caterpillar crawling its way along a twig. She followed it in fascination as it came to the end of the twig, turned itself around and came back.

'Oh look, Granny! He's coming back! He wants to look at me again!'

'That's because you're so beautiful!' I told her.

'That's why I'm looking at *him*. He is so-so-so beautiful!'

I once remarked to a woman I knew quite well how beautiful a basket of citrus fruit looked in a shop window. There were lemons, oranges and grapefruit and limes with a few tomatoes. She stared at me.

'I don't know what you mean,' she said. 'What's beautiful about it?'

Well, I thought, if you can't see it, I can't make you. This is what makes life so enjoyable, being able to see and appreciate such beauty – and all free. I am thankful for the upbringing I had. To love nature and all creation is a legacy I have been able to pass on to my children, grandchildren and now great-grandchildren. I consider myself to be very blessed, having eleven grandchildren and two great-grandchildren – only three girls and the rest all boys. We have had a huge share in their lives. I just love to see the two youngest girls dancing around my living room in their pretty sparkly clothes. They fill the house with laughter and happiness. Over the years, all the charming little boys would lie on their sides as they played with their toy cars, watching the wheels go around and making complementary engine noises. The two little girls, Lexie Rose and Abbie Jay, chatter non-stop and they like me to join in when they thread their beads. Such a simple pleasure, just as I had as a child, and one I had enjoyed playing when I went with my mother to visit Granny in Town.

I smile when I am in Sarah's car and she says, 'Look! There's a kestrel!' (or a red kite or a sparrow hawk). Claire was always very hands-on with nature as a child and she would come home with her pockets full of spiders. Then she would search for the right food to feed them on. We had to try and stop her from keeping things in captivity but it never prevented her from examining every hedgerow to see who or what inhabited the undergrowth.

Shortly after Claire married, she took me into her garden. She had casually fixed a nesting box halfway up her line post. Carefully putting in her hands, she drew out several baby blue tits.

'Oh, Claire! Don't!' I gasped. 'The mother bird might kill them!'

'Oh no,' she said, 'I've been looking at them for ages. The mother bird just perches on the line and watches me. She knows I feed them.'

Well, to my amazement they finally fledged and Claire made a video to prove it.

I remember once sitting on the bus on my way into town. It slowed down and I noticed that many people were staring out of the window. I turned to look and saw a beautiful young girl seated on her bike, waiting for the traffic. Her golden brown hair reached her waist and she wore a fringed suede waistcoat and matching skirt. I saw that it was my daughter Sarah. She saw me and waved. I smiled, and like all proud mothers I wanted to say, 'That's my daughter!' That is how we always think of Sarah. Her name means 'princess' in Hebrew and to all of us who know and love her that is who she is. Her brother and sister are very close to her, as was Virginia when she was alive, and she adored her Granny and Granfer and went on holiday with Mum several times. She helped us cope when we lost our beloved Virginia, spending hours on the phone trying to organise Virginia's legal affairs. She has four children and two grandchildren of her own and lives 'the good life' in Wales, but as my mother used to say, she is only on the end of a phone. I would need dozens of books to do her justice. To us she is a wonderful daughter.

Our son Daniel, Claire's twin, is very calm and quiet, quite the opposite of Claire. He is very clever like his father. There is not much he cannot do. As a little boy he was his father's shadow. He watched and learned. When he was about nine, he made a working radio from bits and pieces John gave him. He proudly took it to school and the teacher allowed him to take it around to show all the other classes. He was a hero that day. He has always been there to help us if he could and he has most recently been a tower of strength when Virginia died abroad. It took all of his fortitude, both mental and physical, and I fear that he may never be the same again. We will always be thankful for our son Dan. Dealing with a family death abroad is traumatic but we all stuck together as a family and drew strength from their support. We are scattered around the globe, but to know that family is there for you in times of trouble is a treasure beyond compare.

I have mentioned my many grandchildren, all dearly loved. My first grandson, James, is in his early thirties now and has one son, Harry James. Harry spent the first year of his life in hospital and has had several operations on his trachea and oesophagus. Despite that he is a happy, charming and bright boy who is a little fighter. It was a very difficult time for his parents, James and Jemma. They spent nearly all their time at the children's hospital for the first year or so, taking care of him themselves. Harry is now on the way to recovery. He is a handsome boy, very much like his Dad. He runs around and gets into all my cupboards; he's a real boy! He still has the tracheotomy in his throat but it doesn't stop him trying to talk. The hardest part of all is not being able to give him a biscuit or a treat as he is still being fed through a tube into his stomach, but that day will come and I am looking forward to it, as is everyone else in the family.

My children and grandchildren have always loved to hear stories from my childhood. Romany life is part of their heritage and makes me who I am. As a family, we always visited the camp regularly. They are still a close family and my cousins Carol and Henry are still living on Granny's bit o' ground, which was bought by Valerie's son.

Our large extended family still have get-togethers. The last one I attended was given by my cousins Bet, Carol and Valerie (Aunt Amy and Uncle Fred's girls) for their brother Henry, who is now eighty. I thought of him as a young lad, making whistles for us out of the withy boughs, and now here he was, a pensioner.

'What a happy man he looks,' I said to John. 'He never married but he's much loved by his sisters and his nephews who have always cared for him. He's always been a kind and gentle man.'

'He doesn't look his age, does he?' John remarked. He is very fond of Henry and loves to chat with him about the good old days. There were dozens of people from the village as well as family. We all had a lovely time and talked about it for days after.

My brother Ted made everyone laugh.

'Our Rosie reminds me of our Aunt Betsy. Always trying to feed me up and offering me cups of tea!'

'Well, that's how we were all brought up!' someone else piped up, 'to be hospitable and to share what we have with family and friends – even the stranger at the door! Even if you have little yourself. That's what brings happiness. Being mean brings misery.'

I have found this to be true, and once learned it cannot be unlearned. We lived by this code and everything we had we shared.

Even now, when the air is still and warm and flowers scent the air, I am at once transported back in time to when I was a tiny child living on Granny's bit o' ground. Dusk always seemed to arrive gently and slowly there. It felt almost magical to a small child. The warm air accentuated the perfume of night-scented stocks and mignonettes. Overlaying this was the perfume of roses hanging heavily on the branches of the old-fashioned pink and white rose briars. Aunt Betsy had given me a handful of dark red plums, still warm from the summer sun. I bent my head, inhaling their sweet smell. In the distance I heard the steam train clickety-clacking over the points, the mournful hoot as the train drew closer. The air stood still and I felt that I was somewhere else and the only person in the world was me. I was completely content. That was one of the most magical moments of my life.

Memories are a lovely thing and a special gift. I see my dear mother with a huge bowl of strawberries in her hands, beaming with pride as she tells me to take them home for our tea. My father with a basket full of fresh vegetables, ''ere you are Rosie,' he would say. 'If it's too much fer yer, share it with yer neighbour.' Then he would stand with his thumbs in his braces making sure that we were safely on our way home and waiting until we were out of sight. I remember being very young, watching a cavalcade of Romany vardoes, horses and dogs running alongside, travelling to who knows where and envying us on Granny's bit o' ground where we would never be moved on. All due to the wisdom and foresight of the wonderful couple we had the privilege to call Granny and Granfer.